Chocolate

Sarah Moss is Assistant Professor of Creative Writing at University College Dublin's School of English, Drama and Film in the Republic of Ireland. She has published six novels as well as a number of non-fiction works. Her work has been nominated three times for the Wellcome Book Prize.

Alexander Badenoch is Assistant Professor in Media and Cultural studies at the University of Utrecht, The Netherlands.

Edible

Series Editor: Andrew F. Smith

Edible is a revolutionary series of books dedicated to food and drink that explores the rich history of cuisine. Each book reveals the global history and culture of one type of food or beverage.

Other Titles in the Series

Cocktails: A Global History by Joseph M. Carlin

Honey: A Global History by Lucy M. Long

Mustard: A Global History by Demet Güzey

Rice: A Global History by Renee Marton

Saffron: A Global History by Ramin Ganeshram

Tea: A Global History by Helen Saberi

Coffee: A Global History by Jonathan Morris

Mango: A Global History by Constance L. Kirker and Mary Newman

Ice Cream: A Global History by Laura B. Weiss

Cheese: A Global History by Andrew Dalby

Chocolate

A Global History

SARAH MOSS
ALEXANDER BADENOCH

MACMILLAN

For Anthony and Kathy

First published in the United Kingdom 2009 by Reaktion Books Ltd
First published in India 2024 by Macmillan
an imprint of Pan Macmillan Publishing India Private Limited
707 Kailash Building
26 K. G. Marg, New Delhi 110001
www.panmacmillan.co.in

Pan Macmillan, The Smithson, 6 Briset St, Farringdon, London EC1M 5NR
Associated companies throughout the world
www.panmacmillan.com

ISBN: 978-93-6113-055-7

1 3 5 7 9 8 6 4 2

Printed and bound in India by Thomson Press India Ltd.

FSC www.fsc.org MIX Paper | Supporting responsible forestry FSC® C010615

Contents

I

Inventing Chocolate

Chocolate is complicated. The 'chocolate tree', *Theobroma cacao*, grows only within twenty degrees of the equator, only below about 1,000 feet (300 m) in altitude. It requires shade, which must be provided by taller trees, and humidity, and a temperature that remains above sixteen degrees Celsius, all of which mean that it does not grow within thousands of miles of the countries that consume the most chocolate. The tree does not take well to being farmed, and is prone to diseases which destroy entire plantations in a few weeks. It depends on midges, which breed best on the floors of uncultivated rainforests, for pollination. The cocoa bean, a pod which grows out of the tree's trunk, must be harvested with a carefully wielded machete to avoid damaging the buds from which more beans will grow, and the process of converting the resultant wrinkly pod into the shiny brown bars we eat is longer and more exact than any other in culinary history, involving a mixture of hand-work and high technology which do not exist in the same economy and, ideally, time spent in at least two climates; the warm, damp environment where it grows and the arid heat required for drying. The chocolate we know is intrinsically modern, the product of a world divided between low-paid manual labour

Cocoa tree.

and mechanized food preparation, between hungry labourers and sleek consumers, and between the ecologically rich Equatorial nations and the economic powers of Europe and North America. It could not exist, in its familiar form, in any other era.

Mesoamerican Chocolate

In the beginning, then, there was no chocolate. There may have been wild *Theobroma cacao* trees in Central America before human beings reached that continent – there were, and are, other species of *Theobroma* – but in any case there is evidence that the tree was domesticated by the earliest civilization of the Americas. Sophie and Michael Coe argue in *The True History of Chocolate* that there is linguistic if not archaeological evidence linking *Theobroma cacao* with the Olmec, the people who inhabited the Mexican Gulf Coast between 1500 and 400 BCE. Partly because of the warm and humid climate which created the fertile lands on which this complex culture was based, little material evidence of Olmec life survives, but traces of cacao have since been found on ceramic vessels from Olmec-era, pre-Classic Maya sites in Belize. Descendants of the Olmec, the Izapan, are the most

Cocoa harvest in West Africa – pods being opened with a small machete.

Mayan stone with relief carving depicting the ruler Itzamna sitting on a throne holding a vision serpent.

likely bearers of cacao to the Maya, whose magnificent cities were established in the cacao-growing lowlands by around 250 CE. It is in the context of the Classic Maya civilization that we begin to encounter the origins of the modern myths of chocolate deployed on wrappers and in the more enthusiastic popular histories.

Both traces and images of Maya cacao consumption survive. Maya writing was decoded in the second half of the twentieth century, and although nearly all of the bark books and codices were destroyed either in the Maya Collapse of the ninth century, when the civilization entered a rapid decline, or by the Spanish in the years following the Conquest, hieroglyphs and pictures on vases attest to cacao use in the Classic era. Many of these vases were found in tests at the Hershey Laboratory in Pennsylvania to contain traces of the chemical theobromine, a component of chocolate that can survive for centuries. Four books survive from the post-Classic era, giving more detail about the first chocolate.

Maya vases depict the harvest, preparation and consumption of chocolate. The beans were picked, fermented and dried near the groves where they grew, after which they could be transported long distances, often up into the highlands, where consumption, at least among the rich, seems to have been untrammelled by distance from the raw material. (The distance between consumers and producers has been

Mayan cacao god.

part of chocolate history from the beginning.) After that, women – it was always women – roasted the beans and then ground them with a pestle, a *mano*, on a flat mortar, a *metate*. A paste of cornmeal was often added at this stage, as well as spices, which might include vanilla, chilli peppers and flower flavourings. The resulting paste was usually diluted to form a drink, which was taken hot or cold, but could also be made into thicker gruels or soups, or even dried to form cakes of 'instant' chocolate which could then be consumed while travelling. Before serving the drink, women would pour it from one container to another until a foam floated on the top.

Many of these vases have been found in graves, and there is usually evidence that they were left full of the prepared drink. The hieroglyphs on these ceramics dedicate the vessel to a god or patron, describe its shape, list the contents and end with a personal name, suggesting that the vases were commissioned by wealthy individuals in readiness for their own burials. Despite its high value, and possible use as a form of currency, cacao was not passed down families and therefore accompanied its owner on the final journey. The hieroglyphics suggest that cacao was involved in rituals for other rites of passage as well as burial, including weddings, anniversaries and celebratory or commemorative banquets. It is easy to see how casual ideas about Mesoamerican history might claim therefore that chocolate was a magic or sacred substance, but we might first reflect on the role of alcohol in our own society: it is not magic, but widely regarded as pleasant and important in marking festivals and social events from 'stag parties' to Holy Communion.

Chocolate took on another function in Mesoamerica. It is often said that the Maya, and later the Aztecs, used cocoa beans as money, as a substitute for gold, and this analogy is presented as an antecedent to our own sense of chocolate's powers. The discovery of fake cocoa beans from Balberta in the first centuries BCE suggests a habit of counterfeiting which would only make sense if the beans were being exchanged for something of value (there is no point in counterfeiting something you are planning to cook), and certainly by the time the Spanish arrived at the Aztec court in 1521, cocoa beans were a recognized way of storing capital. But these events are separated by 1500 years, the distance between now and the decline of the Roman empire, and the meaning and function of the cocoa bean in Mesoamerica cannot have been stable or even consistent across those centuries. Cocoa beans and chocolate lent themselves to exchange because they were grown and produced in specific areas but consumed across the continent and were easily preserved and transported by cargo canoes and in tumplines, backpacks secured by a strap across the forehead. As the Aztec empire, based in what is now Mexico, drew strength after the final throes of the 'Terminal Classic' era of the Maya and the fall of the Toltec people who succeeded them, taxes and tributes were levied in the form of cacao. The Aztec infrastructure was rooted in networks for the passage and exchange of goods, and chocolate was the most portable and widely valued commodity of Mesoamerica.

No-one is sure where the Aztec, or Mexica, people came from, but between the late fourteenth and late fifteenth centuries they established an empire based in Tenochtitlan, the site of the present-day Mexico City. The city throve on tributes exacted from subjugated provinces, and became the powerhouse of a complex and widely misunderstood culture. Later Aztec rulers presided over courts whose hierarchies and etiquettes perhaps find a European equivalent in those of mid-eighteenth-century Versailles.[1] The Aztecs practised a polytheistic religion which was the basis for an advanced

Ancient Mexican drinking cups.

theology, and most of what we know and understand about these disciplines is based on, and thus inevitably shaped by, the accounts of the Spanish conquistadors and their henchmen. Some, especially the Franciscan missionaries of the mid-sixteenth century, learnt Nahuatl and devoted their lives to the study of Aztec culture, but even the most careful records by foreign ethnographers cannot be said, six hundred years later, to give any account of Aztec life that a citizen of pre-Conquest Tenochtitlan might have endorsed. What follows here is an account of the beginnings of European mythmaking about both chocolate and the cultures which originated it.

On 15 August 1502 Columbus had sent his men ashore at Guanaja, an island off modern Honduras, where they had arrived a few days earlier after a traumatic transatlantic passage. The original eyewitness accounts are lost, but Bartolomé de las Casas, working from these lost accounts, writes that, 'as soon as the Governor had gone ashore at this island . . . a canoe full of Indians arrived, as long as a galley and eight feet broad; it came loaded with goods from the west.' These goods included, 'wooden swords . . . certain flint knives, small copper hatchets, and bells and some medals, crucibles to melt the copper; many cacao nuts which they use for money in New Spain, and in Yucatan, and in other parts.' Since these travellers 'did not dare defend themselves nor flee seeing the ships of the Christians', they were taken to the Admiral, who offered gold in exchange for information about local resources. It is Columbus's son Ferdinand who provides the often-quoted detail that this Maya trading canoe was stocked with 'those almonds which in New Spain are used for money. They seemed to hold these almonds at great price; for when they were brought on board ship together with their goods, I observed that when any of these almonds fell, they all stooped to pick it up, as if an eye had fallen.' This is where the equation between chocolate and gold enters the European imagination.

Both Ferdinand Columbus's and Bartolomé de las Casas's accounts of this encounter help to inaugurate the trope in which the 'primitive' people place exaggerated value on something which is, to the eyes of the 'civilized' observer, obviously ephemeral. The people who use nuts as money or value them as if they were eyes anticipate Captain Cook's account of Tahitian excitement over red feathers, or early European accounts of the Native American use of beads. Cacao here is merely a strange plant apparently inscribed with excessive value by people who have not yet encountered the real thing, money. This is a rare glimpse of chocolate before

Theobroma cacao. This nineteenth-century illustration shows the interior of the pod with its sweet pulp and cacao nibs. Note that the fruit grows directly from the trunk of the tree. From *Mathematische und Naturwissenschaften*, by Johann Georg Heck, 1860.

Europeans begin to develop a mythology for it. On this day Guanaja, also known variously at this date as Bonaca and the Island of Pines (Columbus's name for it), began its journey from habitat to source of a luxury comestible. Columbus turned round in search of gold, leaving those who travelled in his wake to discover what those beans were for.

It is no coincidence that the 'most powerful' of the luxury French chocolate manufacturer Valrhona's Grand Cru chocolates, characterized by 'an exceptional bitterness', is called Guanaja. Valrhona state, ambiguously, that Guanaja was 'the first to delight lovers of bitter dark chocolate', leaving us to guess whether this refers to early consumers of the Valrhona bar or those first European visitors to the island. In the pile-up of adjectives that typifies descriptions of fine chocolate in the twenty-first century, Guanaja's 'intense taste brought out by hints of flowers reveals intensity – exceptionally long on the palate.' The consequences of a fleeting encounter on Guanaja that day might well leave a bitter taste.

There were only two years between the first Spanish encounter with the Aztecs in 1519 and the sacking of Tenochtitlan, so what we know about the Aztecs is to a large but indeterminable extent what we know about the Conquistadors. The civilization, including its libraries, was systematically destroyed before any real understanding could have been achieved. But the evidence suggests that great wealth was partnered with sumptuary laws, familiar to medieval Europe, which placed stringent restrictions on luxury even for the upper echelons of a highly stratified society, and that the conspicuous consumption of the court of Moctezuma II (r. 1502–20) was balanced by the ascetic lives of the middle classes. As this suggests, the earliest observers report an ethic of austerity in Aztec society that has been erased from later accounts of debauchery and bloodletting. Chocolate was reserved for those who made the greatest sacrifices to the state, and even then was taken in small quantities at the end of a banquet.

There is relatively little evidence for the association between chocolate and blood. A passage in the Franciscan ethnographer Bernardino de Sahagún's account of Aztec religious ritual, quoted in most histories, suggests that a drink made from cacao and blood-stained water was given to sustain the spirits of sacrificial victims through their final dance, and there was some literary connection between the cocoa bean (which is indeed heart-shaped) and the human heart. One of the traditional ingredients of the chocolate drink, annatto, is also a red food colouring derived from the seeds of the achiote shrub, but it was the Spanish historian and writer Gonzalo Fernández de Oviedo y Valdés (1478–1557) who made the connection between the stained lips of those who had partaken and fresh blood. Again, it is impossible to separate the tensions surrounding first encounters from the cultural peculiarities of cacao in Aztec society,

Aztec polychrome 'waisted' cylindrical vase with 'Palace Scene'.

Aztec vessel, used to hold cocoa, in the shape of a hare.

but some of our own ideas about chocolate's powers and significance are clearly rooted in these earliest anxieties of empire.

Chocolate After Conquest

Historians debate whether new materials from the New World changed European consumers, or whether European consumers assimilated new things as they assimilated alien cultures; how far, in other words, objects retain their foreign identity in the context of colonialism. It is a debate illuminated by the trajectory of chocolate from Aztec luxury to

Native American Indians roasting and grinding the beans, and mixing the chocolate in a jug with a whisk, from John Ogilvy's *America*, 1671.

northern European staple, but in the first decades of this journey it seems that early modern Catholic Europe and declining native Mesoamerican cultures shared ideas about the risks and appropriate use of 'rare victuals'.

The first records of European responses to chocolate are predictably mixed. The Italian historian Girolamo Benzoni, who came across chocolate in Nicaragua in the mid-sixteenth century, thought that 'it seemed more a drink for pigs, than a drink for humanity. I was in this country more than one year, and never wanted to taste it.' Forty years later, the Spanish Jesuit missionary and naturalist José de Acosta wrote that chocolate 'disgusts those who are not used to it, for it has a foam on top, or a scum-like bubbling . . . And the Spanish men – and even more the Spanish women – are addicted to it.' Already, then, there is a distinction in taste between 'proper' Spanish Spaniards and the Creoles, who, while of Spanish birth or extraction, had spent all or most of their lives in South America. Chocolate disgusted the real Europeans, but acculturated men – and especially women – were so far gone as to become 'addicted' to this revolting drink. We might read this as an early account of the 'chocoholic' propensities of women, but alternatively it points to the European fear of 'going native', losing the cultural identity that had brought them to power in the first place, in the outposts of empire. It is the idea of chocolate that is addictive, a potion cooked up by exotic women in the New World.

The association of chocolate with women is enduring. As we have seen, across Mesoamerica chocolate was usually prepared by women, although often consumed by men, and recent work has concluded that, like the British Victorian taste for 'curry', the Spanish liking for chocolate was a result of dependence on native cooks and therefore native cuisine. The missionaries' attempt to fill the social and cultural roles of Aztec priests meant that clerics were also plied with chocolate as they went about their work. In order to govern, the Spanish had to integrate, and part of that integration was the development of a taste for chocolate.

This explains the association of chocolate with native women, but not the insistence that Spanish women took to the drink faster and more enthusiastically than Spanish men. In the mid-seventeenth century the English Dominican Thomas Gage, who celebrated his arrival in Vera Cruz with 'a Cup of the Indian drink called chocolate', told a story of a bishop and the Spanish Catholic women of Chiapas:

> This bishop was (as all the rest are there) somewhat covetous; but otherwise a man of temperate life and conversation, very zealous to reforme whatsoever abuses committed in the Church, which cost him his life before I departed from Chiapa to Guatemala. The women of that

> City it seems pretend much weaknesse and squeamishnesse of stomack, which they say is so great, that they are not able to continue in the Church while a Masse is briefly hudled over, much lesse while a solemn high Masse (as they call it) is sung, and a Sermon preached, unlesse they drinke a cup of hot Chocolatte, and eat a bit of sweetmeats to strengthen their stomacke. For this purpose it was much used by them to make their maids bring to them to the Church in the middle of Masse or Sermon a cup of Chocolatte, which could not be done to all, or most of them without a great confusion and interrupting both Masse and Sermon. The Bishop perceiving this abuse and having given faire warning for the omitting of it, but all without amendment, thought fit to fixe in writing upon the Churches dores an excommunication against all such as should presume at the time of service to eat or drinke within the Church.

Gage and the Prior of the Cathedral tried to calm the bishop, Don Bernardino de Salazar, 'alleadging the custome of the Countrey, the weakenesse of the sex whom it most concerned . . . the contempt that might ensue from them unto his person, and many inconveniencies which might follow to the breeding of an uproar in the church and in the City.' But the bishop was not to be moved, and after there was 'one day such an uproare in the Cathedrall, that many swords were drawn against the Priests and Prebends', the women 'resolved to forsake the Cathedrall', taking with them all the donations and contributions upon which the bishop and his staff depended. In the following month, the bishop fell ill and returned to his cloister, where 'physitians were sent for far and neere, who all with joynt opinion agreed that the Bishop was poysoned.' The bishop died, and

Gage blamed 'a Gentlewoman . . . who was noted to be somewhat too familiar with one of the Bishops Pages', for having 'such a cup of Chocolatte to be ministred by the Page which poysoned him who so rigorously had forbidden Chocolatte to be drunk in the Church.'

This anecdote is sometimes offered as evidence for the addictive properties of chocolate, illustrating that women would choose eternal damnation rather than go without chocolate for a few hours, but in context it is clear that the chocolate is a weapon in a battle between a zealous reforming bishop recently arrived from Spain and the upper classes of a well-established Creole community. Gage goes on to recount his own negotiations with the 'gentlewoman' who sent him chocolate, which he interpreted as thanks for teaching her son Latin and then realised was an unwanted love-offering. 'The women of this City . . . have learned from the Devill many enticing lessons and baits to draw poor soules to sinne and damnation; and if they cannot have their wills, they wil surely work revenge either by Chocolatte or Conserves, or some faire present.' Gage is not writing here about the irresistibility of chocolate but about Spanish suspicion of Creole women and their appetites.

Chocolate-drinking spread steadily through Central American society in the centuries following conquest, and by the late seventeenth century was so widespread that the cultural meanings of cacao multiplied, particularly in relation to gender. Martha Few's work on 'Chocolate, Sex and Disorderly Women in Late-Seventeeth and Early-Eighteenth Century Guatemala' describes a sequence of women accused of using chocolate in poisoning and witchcraft, showing both how strong the association with women of all classes had become and how common the beverage was (the equivalent of the Victorian fear of women who slipped something into their husbands' tea). Juan de Fuentes's allegation to the Inquisition in late seventeenth-century Guatemala that his wife Cecilia had used 'spells and curses' against him provides a neat example of these connections:

> His wife treats him not as a husband but as a servant. He lights the fire in the kitchen, he boils the water, he mixes the chocolate and heats the food . . . and he gets up very early every morning to do this while his wife stays in bed and sleeps until very late. And when his wife wakes, he brings her chocolate so she can drink it after she dresses . . . in this way his wife has turned him into a coward, and all this cannot be a natural thing.

Chocolate, then, was already connected with bad women, women who indulge themselves with mornings in bed instead of attending to their domestic duties. The association between chocolate and feminine 'naughtiness', luxury and self-indulgence that will blossom in modern advertising is already planted, interestingly in the context of a society which, like our own, assumes chocolate to be consumed by most people on most days. Chocolate, in this reading, represents a threatening kind of female eating even as it becomes ubiquitous.

Chocolate was also associated with another kind of moral lapse. Catholics in early modern Europe were enjoined to fast throughout Lent, Pentecost and Advent, as well as most Fridays and every day between midnight and the time of Holy Communion the following day. It was acceptable to allay thirst while fasting, but not to respond to hunger. In an era with highly elaborated ideas about calories, this distinction seems clear, but sixteenth- and seventeenth-century Catholics often drank forms of soup, gruel and egg-nog during these times, which meant that the theological status of chocolate was unclear. Cacao had no stable physical form; as a bean it was compared to almonds, though this may be partly because of the early modern European use of ground almonds as a thickening agent in cooking, which meant that almonds were processed in a way that bears some similarities to the Aztec and Maya handling of cacao. Carried in cakes or slabs on journeys, it was clearly solid food, but dissolved in water it bore more resemblance to gruel or soup (tea and coffee being still unknown). Cacao's cultural functions complicated the issue further, for the Spanish had continued the Aztec custom of levying tributes in the form of cocoa beans, and found that the cacao industry remained profitable under their dispensation. Custom, in any case, outran categorization; as we have seen, Spanish

'The Chocolate', from *Traité nouveau et curieux du café, du thé, et du chocolat* by Philippe Sylvestre Dufour, 1685.

immigrants to Mesoamerica learnt to drink chocolate at all times and in all places before the slow wheels of the Vatican began to work on the relationship between new commodities and fasting.

The result was a period of uncertainty, overlapping with debate about the medical uses and implications of chocolate. If, as some writers suggested, drinking chocolate had enabled Aztec merchants and warriors to march for days without needing any other food or drink, then either that made it ideal for times of fast (because it would facilitate abstention), or it must be absolutely proscribed (because the point of a fast is to suffer). In either case, any substance that had such an effect on the body must have implications for health, perhaps being indicated in the treatment of some diseases or conditions and contraindicated in others. It is in the context of this debate that the first suggestion of chocolate's aphrodisiac properties is made. Although the earliest Spanish observers commented that the Aztec elite consumed chocolate 'for success with women', there is no evidence from any Mesoamerican archaeology, anthropology or surviving codices to substantiate this idea. As Sophie and Michael Coe remark, 'the reader should stop to consider if there has ever been a consumable substance that has not had this reputation at some time and in some place.' Suspicion must be particularly appropriate when the informants are monks vowed to chastity from a culture convinced that all food and drink act to promote or prevent sensual inclinations.

Early modern medicine depended on the Galenic theory of human physiology. Galen was a second-century Greek medical researcher, and his theories as understood by most sixteenth- and seventeenth-century Europeans offered four categories of human physiology, the 'humoural qualities'.

The humours were sanguine, bilious, phlegmatic and melancholic, and individual bodies and personality types were located in relation to these prototypes (and to some extent still are; when we refer to someone as being 'sanguine' about something, or 'full of bile', we mean that they are relaxed or enraged rather than that body fluids are flowing). Dysfunction and disease were usually the result of an imbalance in the humours, and so the aim of treatment was to redress this balance. Drugs played a part, but the distinction between food and medicine is largely a modern one (which may again be dissolving with the interest in nutritional therapies and 'superfoods'), and physicians devoted most of their energies to monitoring and adjusting patients' diets. Just as every body existed in relation to the four categories, so nearly every food acted to heat, cool, moisten or dry the body that consumed it. The relationship between foods and their effects usually appears logical. Strong, spicy flavours such as pepper and the new chillies were hot and dry, associated with bilious tendencies. Strongly flavoured, moist or juicy foods such as meat and wine were linked with blood, and both were given to people who needed strengthening or building up. Subtle, bland flavours, often found in milk and grain-based dishes, promoted cool, phlegmatic habits, while acidic and astringent flavours were 'dry' (like wine or tea) and melancholic. Predictably, hot and moist diets or personalities were associated with sensuality, anger and disorders of excess, while cold and dry people tended to be easy-going or inactive ('cool'), and prone to sadness and declines.

Like most of the new foods from the New World, chocolate did not have an obvious position in this scheme. Taken as a hot drink, especially when flavoured with chilli, chocolate was clearly hot and either moist (because wet) and therefore sanguine, or dry (because of the spices) and therefore bilious.

Many familiar foods occupied two categories within the hot or cold spectra, but the problem with cacao was that it was also thought, in the form of the astringent bean, to be cold and wet, or, as a bitter powder, cold and dry. De Sahagún reported that the Aztecs had used cocoa to treat both fevers and digestive disorders, which in the European understanding would require opposite responses. As with the theological categorization of cacao, it was problematic that practice was far ahead of theory. Everyone was 'taking chocolate' all the time, regardless of its humoural potency, which sometimes made debate appear redundant but also produced an extraordinary range of reported effects. Some people drank chocolate to cool down when they were hot, others to sustain them in fatigue or hard labour. Some people found it helpful in settling the stomach and others in promoting sleep, and most believed that it served their particular purpose. As chocolate usage spread and additional ingredients multiplied, the complexities proliferated. In the end there was a consensus that chocolate should always be taken in moderation and that the effect on the body depended to a large extent on the ingredients and method of preparation, although some writers continued to claim that it was always unhealthy while others regarded it more or less as a panacea. We might observe that categorical advice on healthy eating appears surprisingly elusive.

In several ways, then, modern associations with chocolate can be traced back to the establishment of Spanish colonies in South America. Chocolate, although widely available, connotes women's greed and laziness. While it contains some 'healthy' elements, there is widespread anxiety about the undesirable ways over-indulgence might affect the body. Chocolate also took on another set of meanings which still accompany every mouthful: both the end product and the raw ingredients depended on forced labour. The 'dark history' of sugar, a commodity which was to become inseparable from cacao, is well known, but the production of chocolate depended on the slavery of African labourers two hundred years before the horrors of the Middle Passage entered the European cultural imaginary. Chocolate had always been produced by the poor and consumed by the rich, and chocolate consumers had often lived thousands of miles from the main sites of production in Mesoamerica, but what was new in the seventeenth century was the reliance on an inter-continental slave trade.

Cacao was first grown as a crop, rather than gathered from managed plantations, in the Portuguese settlement of Bahia on the Atlantic coast of Brazil in the seventeenth century. The beans had previously been harvested by Native American groups under the direction of Jesuit missionaries, but with growing demand from the Spanish colonies to the north (the Portuguese in South America never became habitual chocolate consumers) it was apparent that a more intensive system would be profitable. Using the native Tupi as forced labour to gather forastero beans in the rainforest was almost impossible because the Tupi knew the land a great deal better than the missionaries and, since the work was unsupervised, had no difficulty in leaving as and when they wished. The difficulties of working on an industrial scale in the rainforest became overwhelming. Prefiguring the establishment of the sugar and tobacco trades in the following century, the Jesuits switched to managed plantations that were serviced almost entirely by slaves from the Portuguese colonies in West Africa. The enduring advantage of cacao rather than sugar or tobacco in this context was that the processes involved were so complicated as to provide work for children, women in advanced pregnancy and the elderly as well as the strong adults needed for heavy work in the fields. Cacao facilitated the use (abuse) of slave labourers from cradle, or at least toddlerhood, to grave. As the market expanded with the European acquisition of the taste for chocolate, a number calculated at 'nearly ten percent of the volume of the whole transatlantic slave trade' went to work on the cacao plantations in Brazil.

2
The Chocolate House

Chocolate entered Europe through Spain late in the sixteenth century. For chocolate to make this transatlantic passage, there had to be consumers in Spain who knew that they wanted it, and in this light the lapse of seventy years between the first European encounter with cacao and the presence of chocolate drinks in monasteries and at the court of King Philip II is not surprising. Monks and merchants had to travel to the New World, remain there long enough to acquire a taste for new commodities, and return to Spain for long enough to introduce these commodities to their social networks. Monastic orders provided networks which reached across the Atlantic but also across Europe, and the Jesuits and Dominicans were initially responsible for the dissemination of chocolate in the Old World.

The first records of cocoa in Europe portray a substance of value only because it was exotic, a curiosity from the New World that came in a literal package with striking feathers from strange birds and copal incense. A group of Kekchi Maya nobles brought to the Spanish court by Dominican missionaries brought prepared chocolate as part of their official offering, and when representatives of the religious orders in South America attended convocations in Europe, they took with them 'great wealth and gifts to the Generalls, to the Popes and Cardinals and Nobles in Spain, as bribes to facilitate whatsoever just or unjust, right or wrong they are to demand.'[2] By the first decades of the seventeenth century, chocolate and the paraphernalia used in its consumption in the Spanish American colonies were regularly included in transatlantic shipments of goods, albeit in quantities suggesting private consumption among the elite rather than the development of a metropolitan Spanish market.

Chocolate was consumed in Europe in much the same form as in Mesoamerica for at least the first half of the seventeenth century. The traditional chocolate spices, vanilla, chilli, the colourant annatto and 'ear flowers' (*Cymbopetalum penduliflorum*) were all imported with the cacao, which usually came in its solid, processed form. As several still lifes from the period demonstrate, chocolate drinkers in Spain used the

Chocolate cup, Petit Palais Musée des Beaux-Arts, Paris.

Women grinding cocoa, from E. G. Squier's *Nicaragua*, 1852.

jícara, a laminated gourd used as a chocolate cup in pre-Conquest Tenochtitlan, or the clay *tecomate*, as drinking vessels. The foam on the top of the drink was valued as much by Spanish consumers as it had been by the Aztecs or indeed the Maya, and the practice of making it with a whisk called a *molinillo* rather than by pouring from a height went back at least to the first years of the colony.

As years passed and chocolate became more widespread in Spain and then Italy, substitutions were made by those who could not find or afford the authentic seasonings or impedimenta. The honey used for sweetening in Mesoamerica would sometimes be replaced with sugar, and more readily available spices from the Middle East such as pepper and cinnamon began to take the place of chilli. Rose petals or oils were used in place of the Amazonian 'ear flowers' and musk might be added, perhaps both to accentuate the luxury status of chocolate and to mimic the aromatic qualities of the Mesoamerican preparation. Sometimes, perhaps in memory of the maize thickeners used in chocolate on ordinary occasions in sixteenth- and seventeenth-century Mesoamerica, the Spanish added almonds or eggs and milk to their chocolate drinks, which were usually but not always taken hot. There are directions for processing cocoa beans from raw in a domestic kitchen dating from the end of the seventeenth century, but most cacao probably arrived in its most stable form, as solidified cakes requiring only to be dissolved for drinking.

Chocolate remained characteristically Spanish until the end of the seventeenth century, although English and Italian friars had encountered it in New Spain a hundred years earlier. Chocolate was served to both inquisitors and victims of the Inquisition, including at public scenes of torture and execution, and was regarded by visitors as a speciality of the Spanish court. An Italian medical treatise of the mid-1600s makes reference to cocoa, but the first reliable evidence of chocolate being prepared and drunk outside Spain is from the court of Grand Duke Cosimo III of Tuscany, where toasted cocoa beans were crushed and infused with jasmine flowers before being ground with sugar, vanilla and ambergris, which is a floral-smelling intestinal accretion of the sperm whale. At around the same date, the court of Louis XIII of France was served by two Italian cooks, who brought with them coffee, chocolate and tea. It was Louis XIV's marriage to the Spanish Infanta Maria Theresa in the 1660s that brought a retinue of habitual chocolate drinkers to the court of the Sun King, from where Madame de Sévigné famously wrote to her daughter, marooned in the provinces, about the newly fashionable beverage.

England in the second half of the seventeenth century might have been expected to afford less of a welcome to an expensive novelty from the courts of Catholic Europe. In 1642 the reign of Charles I collapsed into a civil war in which Charles was routinely identified with loose-living Continental Absolutist monarchs, in contrast to the Protestant clean living that his opponent Oliver Cromwell claimed to exemplify. The dominant, although contested, Puritan ethos regarded luxury, indulgence and sensuality as sinful, and rejected several foodstuffs on this principle. (It was Cromwell who is popularly said to have outlawed Christmas pudding as an inappropriate way of marking Jesus' assumption of mortality.) At the same time, war – as ever – required increased ingenuity in the kitchen and also increased mobility among soldiers and those fleeing the country or their enemies, accelerating exposure to and use of new ingredients. The cookbooks which began to appear in the 1650s, after the end of the civil war, in fact display a thirst for new, foreign flavours and recipes. Edward Phillips's 1658 *The New World of English Words, or, A General Dictionary Containing the Interpretations of such Hard Words as are Derived from Other Languages*, defines chocolate as 'a compounded Indian drink, whose chief ingredient is a fruit called Cocao'. It seems that the first chocolate houses, semi-public spaces more seemly than ale houses but more sociable than drinking at home, were established in London in the late 1650s. A flyer for M. Sury's chocolate house 'neare East gate', published in Oxford in 1660, only ten years after the opening of the first English coffee house in the same city, is misleadingly titled 'The vertues of the chocolate East-India drink'. This pamphlet promises prospective customers that 'By this pleasing drink health is preserved, sicknesse diverted, It cures Consumptions and Cough of the Lungs; it expels poison, cleanseth the teeth, and sweetneth the Breath; provoketh Urine; cureth the stone

The gaming room at White's chocolate house, from Hogarth's *The Rake's Progress*, 1735.

and strangury, maketh Fatt and Corpulent, faire and aimeable, it cureth the running of the Reins, with sundry other desperate Diseases.' The writer bursts into verse to explain the benefits to women:

Nor need the Women longer grieve,
Who spend their oyle yet not Conceive,
For 'tis a Help Immediate,
If such but Lick of Chocolate.

The Nut-Browne Lasses of the Land,
Whom Nature vail'd in Face and hand,
Are quickly Beauties of High-Rate,
By one small Draught of Chocolate.

Many expensive and/or exotic substances were said to cure female infertility and promote beauty; one should probably not read too much into the attribution of these particular qualities to chocolate, but it is interesting that the stuff is advertised for its effects rather than its taste. Chocolate, like coffee in these decades, was still more part of the *materia medica* than an ingredient for domestic cooks. This is not to say that it was always taken, like modern prescribed drugs, to redress a particular problem, but was rather consumed to promote particular kinds of well-being, like drinking camomile tea before bed or espresso before work.

Despite the rhyme on the Oxford flyer, chocolate was still consumed in seventeenth-century England mostly by men in the largely homosocial environment of chocolate houses. It used to be said that coffee-house culture was exclusively masculine, but although certainly the great majority of customers were men it is now clear that women owned and worked in the famous London coffee houses from their beginnings in the late seventeenth century until they were reincarnated as private clubs in the nineteenth century. There is no reason to believe that the shorter-lived chocolate houses were any different. The references to chocolate in Samuel Pepys's diary place it squarely in this context; the first mention is in January 1660, when someone leaves 'a Quantity of Chocolate' at his house as a gift, but thereafter chocolate is an unquestioned part of the world of the upwardly mobile politician and intellectual that Pepys exemplifies. On 24 April 1661 Pepys wakes, 'with my head in a sad taking through the last night's drink, which I am very sorry for; so rose and went out with Mr Creed to drink our morning draft, which he did give me in chocolate.' On 17 October 1662 Pepys, who made a great career in naval administration, discussed his successes with Lord Sandwich and then went

Martin Engelbrecht, *The Chocolate Drink*, *c.* 1740.

> with Mr Creed to Westminster Hall, and by and by thither comes Captn. Ferrers, upon my sending for him, and we three to Creed's chamber, and there sat a good while and drank chocolate. Here I am told how things go at Court; that the young men get uppermost, and the old serious lords are out of favour; that Sir H. Bennet, being brought into Sir Edward Nicholas's place, Sir Charles Berkeley is made Privy Purse; a most vicious person, and one whom Mr Pierce, the surgeon, today (at which I laugh to myself), did tell me that he offered his wife £300 per annum to be his mistress.[3]

Chocolate is what professional men with powerful positions at court and in government drank while exchanging news. In this light, chocolate's role in late seventeenth-century England seems more like its role in pre-Conquest Tenochtitlan than either early modern Mesoamerica or Louis XIV's Versailles.

Early in the eighteenth century, recipes using chocolate as an ingredient began to appear in English cookbooks. At first there are instructions for making the drink served in chocolate houses at home, which give a sense of how much conventions had changed since the Spanish began to replicate Moctezuma's ceremonial drink at home. *The Accomplish'd Female Instructor*, published in London in 1704, gives this recipe:

> To make Chocolate the best way.
>
> Take an equal Proportion of Water and Milk, let them well incorporate in Boyling, but continually stir them, lest they burn to the Bottom; so having grated or beaten your Chocolate Cakes fine, put to a Quart of the Liquor an Ounce and a half or two Ounces, if you would have it rich, then take it off the Fire, and put to it two

> Yolks of new lay'd Eggs well beaten up with as much fine Sugar dissolved in Rose-water, as will sweeten it; then mill it with a Milling-stick, till it becomes thick, and so pour it into dishes.

This drink – or perhaps, given the egg yolks, custard – is well on the way to modern 'hot chocolate'. The spices are gone, replaced by rose water, which may represent the ghost of the Maya 'ear flowers' but is a standard ingredient of English sweet dishes from the beginning of the sixteenth century. Milk has joined water as the base of the drink, perhaps because of the egg thickener. But sugar is still added to taste and the Spanish *molinillo* survives in the 'Milling-stick'. The cakes, of course, are not chocolate cake as we would now recognize it, but cacao in its solid, processed form. It is easy to see how, within a decade or two of entering the domestic kitchen, this hybrid became a dessert. Similar ingredients are combined in two different ways in early eighteenth-century English cookery. Recipes for 'Chocolate Cream' dissolve chocolate in a little boiling water and then add a pint of cream and two eggs per quarter pound of chocolate, beat it until it boils, allow it to cool, and then beat it again 'that it may go up with a Froth'. This is in the old English tradition of creams and syllabubs. The alternative is a kind of macaroon. The second edition of Mary Kettilby's *Collection of Above Three Hundred Receipts in Cookery, Physic and Surgery; For the use of All Good Wives, Tender Mothers, and Careful Nurses*, published in London in 1719, includes 'Lemon or Chocolate-Puffs':

> Take half a pound of Double-refin'd Sugar, finely beat and sifted, grate into it the yellow rind of a very fair large Lemon; then whip up the White of an Egg to a froth, and

> wet it with this froth, 'till 'tis as stiff as a good working Paste, lay it on Papers and bake it in a very slow Oven; lay some round and some long: If you make Chocolate, grate about an ounce as you did the Peel.

Chocolate had begun to be used in Italian cookery two or three decades earlier. Elizabeth David, in *Harvest of the Cold Months: A Social History of Ice and Ices* (1994), describes a household management book by Antonio Latini published in Naples in the early 1690s, which gives a recipe for – or perhaps account of – a chocolate sorbet. Equal weights of unsweetened chocolate and sugar were beaten with approximately three times their combined weight in water and 'worked or stirred, it would seem from Latini's hazy instructions, during the whole of the freezing process. The mousse was to be served as soon as it was frozen.' Like the chocolate creams and 'puffs', this sorbet would have been served as part of the dessert course, meant for spectacle more than nourishment, which appeared as the grand finale of the most formal meals and banquets in the seventeenth and early eighteenth centuries. The presence of these dishes in cookbooks signals that they were available at least as objects of aspiration to those of the gentry who, unable to afford fully trained professional cooks who would not have needed written recipes, were nevertheless willing to invest in expanding their own tastes (at least in theory, since it is by no means obvious that people who buy cookbooks cook and eat the dishes in them). These are class-specific, and they are also, of course, distinctively European creations which would have been unrecognizable in Mesoamerica.

Drinking chocolate became an established part of the eighteenth-century breakfast in France and England, but recipes for chocolate cakes, tarts, mousses and creams also proliferated. When the English dined at midday, as most did until the late seventeenth century, breakfast seems to have been an informal snack of whatever leftovers were around. Dinner, especially for the aristocracy, became steadily later through the eighteenth century, eventually displacing 'supper' (previously taken before retiring to bed) and creating a vacancy for what became 'lunch'. A later dinner meant that there was more emphasis on breakfast, which became a meal

Pietro Longhi, *Morning Chocolate*, *c.* 1750.

Georg David Matthieu, *Seated Portrait of Herzogin Louise Friederike zu Mecklenburg-Schwerin opening a letter*, 1770s.

in itself rather than a way of getting by until dinner, and the upper classes took to convening at ten in the morning to eat various kinds of bread, toast and plain cakes accompanied by coffee or chocolate. It is in this context that beautiful silver and porcelain chocolatieres were produced. Like coffee pots, except that they still had holes in the lids for the *molinillo* or milling-stick, these chocolatieres are often shown in mid-eighteenth-century family portraits, as if they represent the temperate sociability of the Georgian aristocratic ideal. His friend Hester Thrale Piozzi's account of Samuel Johnson's use of chocolate illustrates the idea of the chocolatiere as the centrepiece of morally improving domestic conversation. She writes:

> With regard to drink, his liking was for the strongest, as it was not the flavour, but the effect, he sought for . . . For the last twelve years, however, he left off all fermented liquors. To make himself some amends, indeed, he took his chocolate liberally, pouring in large quantities of cream, or even melted butter; and was so fond of fruit, that though he usually ate seven or eight large peaches of a morning . . . and treated them with proportionate attention after dinner, yet I have heard him protest that he never had quite as much as he wished of wall-fruit.

Chocolate here works as an interesting replacement for 'the strongest drink', one which is associated with the insatiable appetite for the rare luxury of peaches. Hot-house and wall-grown fruit were available only to those who commanded substantial estates and skilful gardeners, so to say that one could not get enough wall-fruit would be like regretting the lack of alpine strawberries or quail's eggs. Chocolate, or at

Jean-Baptiste Charpentier, *The Penthievre Family, or the Cup of Chocolate*, 1768.

Jean-Etienne Liotard, *The Chocolate Girl*, *c.* 1743–5.

least chocolate with the excessive enrichment of cream and butter, seems to come close to this category.

As this vignette suggests, the orderly domesticity of the leisured families gathered around chocolatieres in eighteenth-century portraiture is not always reflected in the literature of the period. From the writings of the Marquis de Sade at one extreme to those of Jane Austen at the other, chocolate in later eighteenth-century literature is almost invariably associated with a degenerate, loose-living aristocracy, addicted to luxury and oblivious to the suffering of the poor. (This could, of course, be the view from the other side of the silk-clad families enjoying their slave-grown chocolate of a morning.) It is here that we see chocolate being feminized in England after its association with the distinctly masculine environment of the coffee house in the seventeenth century.

Histories of chocolate often cite the gastronomic tastes of the Marquis de Sade as evidence of chocolate's innately erotic appeal. De Sade's fiction involves the frequent consumption of chocolate before and during sexual orgies, and his letters to his wife, usually from prison, contain repeated, urgent requests for all kinds of confectionery. The interest in chocolate in the pornographic fiction is explicitly related to coprophagy, and a strand of chocolate scholarship explores this relationship in more detail, but in fact when de Sade was grooming prostitutes in real life he tended to give them confections containing aniseed and, allegedly, the aphrodisiac cantharides (Spanish fly) in order to provoke lust and wind. There is little evidence that either was effective, and indeed little evidence that de Sade's practises bore much relation to his fiction. De Sade's prison letters to his wife make many demands for clean linen, particular toiletries and all sorts of cakes and sweets. On 16 May 1779, he upbraids Madame de Sade for failing to fulfil his order:

> The sponge cake is not at all what I asked for. 1st, I wanted it iced all over, underneath and on top, with the same icing as the little cakes; 2nd I wanted it to have chocolate inside, and there isn't even the least trace of chocolate. I beg you to have it sent to me at the first opportunity, and make sure that someone trustworthy puts the chocolate in. The cakes must smell of it, as if you're biting into a bar of chocolate.

On 15 June 1783 he writes:

> First of all I need linen, very definitely, or I'm out of here; four dozen meringues, two dozen big cakes; four dozen vanilla pastilles with chocolate, and not an unspeakable drug like the one you sent before.[4]

Any relationship between chocolate and sex here is clearly one of substitution. The combination of specificity and sensuality, the precision about both how the cake should be iced and how it should feel to smell it, recalls de Sade's highly organized approach to debauchery in *Les 120 Journées de Sodome*. But it is worth noting that, as devotees of rare and expensive chocolate usually point out, those who 'need' chocolate usually need it in a very sugary form. De Sade is not asking for the best South American cocoa, or demanding a chocolatiere or a *molinillo*. He wants 'biscuit de Savoie', a fat-free sponge cake, with a great deal of icing, and then he wants meringues, cakes and vanilla and chocolate candies, foods that require time, expertise and effort to produce. De Sade's irritation with the inadequacies of previous care packages emphasizes his impotence and frustration in these transactions. These requests are reminiscent of the fantasies of lost polar explorers or the protagonists of children's fiction, people for whom food displaces the normal adult interests in money and sex. Food histories tend to quote the paragraphs about chocolate, but de Sade also demands gloves, powder, toiletries, candles (different sizes for different times of day) and books. It's not about chocolate but about power and gratification behind bars, and if chocolate offers one of several ways of exercising this power it is because, like the other commodities, it signifies class. De Sade requires his wife to send him the trappings of aristocratic life in late eighteenth-century France, to prove her enduring loyalty despite his disgrace and so he can prove that, regardless of the convictions for rape, sodomy and assault and the growing certainty of a life of incarceration, he is still a Marquis of the *ancien régime*.

De Sade is an extreme case, but the association of chocolate with the personal and political sins of the aristocracy in the late eighteenth century is strong. The beginning of Frances Burney's second novel, *Cecilia*, establishes the heroine's status as 'heiress to an estate of 3000 pounds per annum', 'the accumulating possessions of a rising and prosperous family'. Since we meet Cecilia at the breakfast given to mark her departure from her childhood home, the first chapter has to work hard and fast to equip the heroine with all she requires to remain aristocratic in the reader's mind through the hundreds of pages of tribulations that follow. Chocolate forms part of this shorthand, as the foolish Mr Morrice 'studious to recommend himself' to the wealthy orphan and 'indifferent by what means', 'eagerly offered to assist her with cakes, chocolate, or whatever the table afforded'. In Jane Austen's novels of upper middle-class life it is only the very rich and autocratic General Tilney who drinks chocolate, while Caroline Austen's reminiscences of life at Steventon Rectory suggest the correct estimate of chocolate. Looking back from the 1870s, Caroline remembers her sister Anna's wedding:

> The breakfast was such as the best breakfasts then were: some variety of bread, hot rolls, buttered toast, tongue or ham and eggs. The addition of chocolate at one end of the table, and the wedding cake in the middle, marked the specialty of the day.[5]

And after that, the bride and groom set off for their new home. Chocolate and wedding cake, neither of which were to be consumed without proper reason, were enough to mark the occasion without vulgarity.

At the same time as art and literature in northern Europe presented chocolate as an integral part of aristocratic life, associated at least as fully with its vices as with its virtues, there were two developments towards the democratization

François Boucher, *The Breakfast*, 1739.

of chocolate which would characterize its nineteenth century history. Chocolate production began to be mechanized and chocolate re-crossed the Atlantic, beginning to be consumed and then produced in North America.

Most of the cocoa consumed in Europe was ground by hand, possibly until as late as the nineteenth century, although a watermill had been used for cocoa in 1729. In cities across Europe, chocolate grinders carried their *metates*, not significantly different from those used by the Maya, from one house to another, kneeling to grind the roasted beans with stone rollers. It was work particularly associated with Sephardic Jews, who suffered waves of persecution at the hands of the trade guilds that policed food production in Europe until the late eighteenth century. In 1761 Joseph Fry of Bristol expanded his chocolate sales following the purchase of a watermill, and three years later had a London warehouse and 'a network of agents in fifty-three towns'. By the late 1770s there were water-powered chocolate workshops in several French towns, and at the end of the century eight German and Austrian cities claimed chocolate factories. Dutch producers, naturally, used windmills, while there was a mule-driven mill in Spain; the idea of using inanimate power to grind large quantities of grain or beans had long been familiar, and as soon as steam power was available, it was applied to cocoa beans as well as wheat.

It is in the context of these processes that it becomes possible to trace chocolate consumption in North America. Relatively little is known about cocoa in colonial North America, but it seems to have reached the colony mostly via import from Britain (although this seems highly unlikely given the obvious probability of overland trade with Central American producers). Cocoa shipments were very heavily taxed, which makes it probable that rather more chocolate entered

Early factory methods.

the colony than was officially recorded. Despite high prices, coffee houses in Boston in the late seventeenth century served chocolate, and there are records of artisans and labourers possessing cocoa beans. Account books from mid-eighteenth-century shops show individual merchants ordering small supplies of cocoa from England, along with sugar, tea and coffee. There were *metates* in colonial America, but most consumers bought chocolate in blocks which, by the end of the eighteenth century, were manufactured in the East Coast cities. As in Britain, chocolate was supplied to soldiers as a portable and dense source of energy, and it was consumed by fighters on both sides during the American Revolution.

The first documented chocolate mill in North America began to turn in 1765, when John Hannan, an Irish emigrant chocolate maker, began to work on the Neponset River in Dorchester, Massachusetts (although given the presence of mills in most American towns in this era, it seems likely that some of them occasionally ground cocoa as well as grain). In 1779 John Hannan disappeared, having said that he was investigating cocoa suppliers in the West Indies, and the following year James Baker took over the business. Under his son, Edmund, trade expanded rapidly when imports from Europe collapsed during the 'War of 1812', and in 1824 James Baker's grandson Walter took charge. Now owned by the Kraft corporation, Baker's chocolate is still widely available in North America.

Despite the rise and rise of American chocolate cookery upon which Baker's continues to depend, chocolate in America seems to have remained almost exclusively the basis of an expensive drink until the nineteenth century. Early American cookbooks make no use of chocolate as an ingredient, and there seems to be no parallel to the idea of chocolate as an aristocratic women's luxury which kept European chocolate in its place until the technological advances of the nineteenth century replaced the spicy, bitter beverage with a sweet milky substance bearing minimal resemblance to the chocolates of Mesoamerica.

3
The Chocolate Factory

Chocolate became increasingly mobile in the eighteenth century, but continued to flow into Europe from one source: Spanish and Portuguese colonies in South America. In the nineteenth century, this dynamic changed. Chocolate began to be grown, manufactured and produced in new locations, places to which *Theobroma cacao* was neither botanically nor culturally native. As the empires of the nineteenth and twentieth centuries took shape, chocolate began to flow in new channels and took on new meanings. Like much of our modern material culture, it also underwent a profound transformation during the nineteenth century. It entered the 1800s as a fatty drink and ended them as (among many other things) the mass-produced milky drink and solid bar familiar to consumers today. The firms that first mobilized the innovations in production, commodification and marketing that underpinned this transformation are mostly still the major players in the industry today. Chocolate began as product associated (in Europe) with Catholic clergy and idle, languid aristocracy, and ended its transformation being sold as a dietary staple and nutritious boon to the working poor. In the process it became associated with places from African jungles to alpine meadows, and identified with everything from maternal love to purple cows.

The eminent historian Eric Hobsbawm describes the last two centuries as consisting of a 'long' nineteenth century, stretching from the French Revolution in 1789 to the outbreak of the First World War in 1914, and a 'short' twentieth century, which lasted from the First World War and the Russian Revolution until the collapse of the Soviet Union in 1991. If we measure historical time (as people sometimes measure their days) by chocolate, the dates are somewhat different, but similar periods could be said to apply. The chocolate nineteenth century began not so much with the storming of the Bastille as with the related wars of independence in South America, which interrupted a number of the supply chains of cacao, and set in motion a transformation of production. The end of the chocolate century came not so much with the First World War, which put barely a dent in expansion and production, but with the profound disruption of most global commerce, and particularly decolonization, in the wake of the Second World War. And if we consider the end of forced labour in the chocolate industry as one of the markers of the nineteenth century, in some places it has yet to end.

Revolutions, and the Lack Thereof

Revolutionary stirrings in the late eighteenth century had an impact on both sides of the chocolate chain. Throughout the Caribbean, Napoleon's conquest of Spain and Portugal in 1806 sparked already militant opposition to Spanish authority into open rebellion, which reached a peak in the Venezuelan revolution in 1811, and spread throughout the northern part of the continent. Many of these revolts were led by the Creole elite there, who owned most of the cacao plantations. They wanted both freedom from Spain and to strengthen their hold over the territories to avoid slave rebellions such as the one that had happened in Haiti a few years earlier. Ironically, Venezuela did indeed gain independence, but in the process many of the planters lost their slaves (who in many cases were recruited into the loyalist armies) and/or their plantations. Due to this unrest and lack of cheap labour, production of cacao in South America declined sharply, and only recovered much later in the century, when newly independent nations such as Ecuador came once more into their own as chocolate suppliers.

Along with production in Central and South America (where consumption among all classes remained common), consumption of chocolate in Europe also declined sharply during the Napoleonic wars. The various naval blockades of the continent limited the import of chocolate to most parts of Europe, after the initial destruction of the Spanish fleet that had once brought most of the cacao across the Atlantic. After the end of the war in Europe, chocolate supplies remained low because reduced incomes meant reduced demand and because continued unrest in South American affected production. Chocolate remained an expensive luxury for several decades.

In many places, expensive chocolate was replaced by other drinks. Unlike cacao, coffee and tea could still find their way into Europe via the 'back door' of Asia in spite of blockades, and they were generally cheaper to come by. A very wide array of local products were produced to replace the popular but now scarce hot drinks. Salep, a drink made from roasted orchid roots, once popular throughout the Ottoman empire, began to be produced locally and enjoyed renewed popularity in Britain as chocolate and other hot drinks became unavailable or prohibitively expensive in the first decades of the century. Like chocolate, and unlike coffee or tea, salep was thick and considered very nutritious. The root of the chicory plant was similarly roasted and brewed as a drink. Many of these drinks were common for many years after their colonial counterparts became available once more, usually among the poorer classes. Chicory, for example, grew

A cacao press of the kind pioneered by Van Houten in 1828.

popular in Germany during the continental blockades and only went fully out of mainstream taste there at the end of scarcity several wars later, when 'real bean coffee' came into the financial reach of all socio-economic groups in the early 1950s. It remains a tradition in many places, including India and, perhaps more famously, New Orleans.

The decline of chocolate production and consumption in the early nineteenth century was the first and perhaps only interruption in a steady expansion from the sixteenth century to the present day. It was during this decline that the manufacturing development which allowed chocolate to take on its familiar, modern form occurred. Chocolate had such a high fat content that the excess cocoa butter had to be skimmed off the finished drink or absorbed in starchy additions such as arrowroot, potato starch or sago flour. In 1828 the Dutch Coenraad van Houten developed a process for using a hydraulic press to extract cocoa butter from chocolate liquor. Using this press, he was able to reduce the cocoa butter content of the liquor from 53 per cent to around 27 per cent, leaving a cake that could easily be powdered and sold for drinking. In addition, van Houten then took the additional step of adding alkaline salts (the process now known as 'Dutching', as it became standard practice first in Dutch cocoa manufacture), which improved the way the chocolate mixes with water, in addition to making its flavour milder and its colour darker.

Nearly every history of chocolate, not least the potted histories now put forward by chocolate manufacturers themselves, lists this 1828 event as a major turning point in chocolate history, and gives the impression that a revolution in form and mass production of chocolate took off soon after. This has more to do with our habits of telling history as a story of heroic inventors and technological transformations, however, than it does with the ways and forms of chocolate in the nineteenth century. Van Houten's press did not come out of the blue: there had been experiments with cocoa butter presses since the late seventeenth century. What is more, while van Houten's press eventually did play an important role in chocolate manufacture, its immediate impact, both on van Houten's fortunes particularly and chocolate production generally, was negligible. For many years to come, even people in van Houten's native Netherlands still prepared the drink from pressed bars of unsweetened, fully fatted chocolate and boiling water. In fact, more 'traditional' ways of preparing and consuming chocolate persisted in a number of places alongside the increasing number of new and now more familiar forms of chocolate that emerged over the course of the century.

Instead of looking at van Houten's invention as a revolutionary event, looking at it in context provides a neat illustration of the actual state of chocolate production and consumption in Europe at the time. The main reason this supposed 'revolution' was mostly ignored at first is that there was very little use for the excess cocoa butter. At that point the only useful by-product of chocolate production was the shells. These were ground and used roasted as a cheap tea-like drink, which was consumed by lower classes in the Low Countries and Ireland (where it was known as 'miserables'). The shells were also used for animal fodder or used illicitly as a filling agent in pressed chocolate to stretch the more expensive product. Extracting the cocoa butter was thus primarily a more efficient means of making the drink less fatty, but it did not generate any useful by-products.

Van Houten's development was one part of a wave of mechanization and industrialization of chocolate production, in which not the Dutch but the French were at the forefront.

Already in the early part of the century, a number of individual chocolate manufacturers in France were mechanizing chocolate production, adding machines to the processes of grinding. This was one area where van Houten's press did have more immediate impact, but not in the way or place that one might expect. J. M. Lehmann of Dresden, who had helped van Houten develop his hydraulic press, went into business in 1834 specializing in cocoa processing machinery and soon became one of the leading manufacturers throughout Europe. British manufacturers Cadbury Brothers of Birmingham and J. S. Fry & Sons bought presses in 1860 and 1866 respectively. Furthermore, it was Lehmann's machines that the American candy-maker Milton Snavely Hershey saw on display at the World's Columbian Exposition of 1893 in Chicago. Once the exhibition closed, Hershey bought the machines and they became the cornerstone of his new chocolate business.

Finally, although van Houten's press was not an immediate success, the fact that he was investing in chocolate production at a time when chocolate supposedly 'suffered from an unfashionable image' is also worthy of note. Clearly there was enduring demand for chocolate, *ancien régime* or insecurity of supply notwithstanding. The renowned French gastronome Jean Anthelme Brillat-Savarin wrote in 1825 that chocolate 'had become completely ordinary' in France, particularly after the blockades ended and 'rid us of all those humbugs one was forced to taste, but which were no more chocolate than chicory is mocha.' Indeed, Brillat-Savarin had nothing but praise for the substance, emphasizing particularly its healthy qualities:

> It remained for time and experience, those two great masters, to show that chocolate prepared with care is as healthy as it is agreeable. That it is nourishing, easily digested, and

> is not so injurious to beauty as coffee is said to be. It is very suitable for those persons who are given to great mental toil, to professors and lawyers, especially to travellers. It also suits certain feeble stomachs, and has been thought most advantageous in chronic diseases. It is the last resource in ailments of the pylorus.

Brillat-Savarin's descriptions of chocolate illustrate the new social structure in which chocolate was circulating. While he emphasizes the overall nutritious nature of chocolate, he also makes abundantly clear that its benefits are really only available to those who possess the skills to prepare it properly, and the bodily discipline to know when and how to take it. The renewed emphasis on the health benefits of chocolate seems to fit in well at a time when a taste for it was certainly widespread, but there was general uncertainty about the correct forms of preparation and consumption. This also highlights the ambiguous position between confection and medicine that chocolate would still occupy through much of the century.

For the first half of the century, then, the meanings and physical form of chocolate were shifting. In a number of local settings, confectioners and pastry-makers – in addition to pharmacists – were creating novelties they could sell, and chocolate was one of the ingredients that seemed to show promise. The innovations that slowly transformed chocolate took place not in the Netherlands, but first in Britain, then in Switzerland, much later in the century. In Britain, the firm of J. S. Fry & Sons pioneered the creation of a solid chocolate by pressing out and then reintroducing some of the cocoa butter. The result was more moist than the solid pastilles which had been sold until then, but remained somewhat gritty and was not very popular. Swiss manufacturers were also experimenting with ways to produce solid chocolate confections more cheaply and palatably to meet the expanding demand. Small merchants, whose names are well-known firms or brands now such as François-Louis Cailler (whose name now graces Nestlé's quality range) and Philippe Suchard (another enduring industry name), began to perfect mechanical processes for grinding and mixing superior chocolate. The great Swiss breakthroughs came in 1879. One of them was the invention of milk chocolate in the form we know it now. Cailler's son-in-law and heir in the chocolate business, Daniel Peter, devised a system for combining the powdered milk recently invented by his countryman Henri Nestlé with chocolate (Nestlé bought the Cailler, Peter, Kohler firm in 1929). The result, which also utilized cocoa butter, formed an easily moulded solid. Independently, Rodolphe Lindt came up with a mechanical process known as 'conching', in which granite rollers manipulate the chocolate liquor, mixing and heating it gently, resulting in a smooth mass and better flavour. This resulted in the sort of chocolate with which we are now familiar – a smooth-grained solid substance for eating – and made Lindt's fortunes; to this day, Lindt & Sprüngli are an independent and well-known firm. Many other firms soon picked up the technique – that is, purchased the machine – and slowly the new form diffused. Both of these forms also came up with a use for cocoa butter, which is reintroduced once it is pressed out. It was this use, and later on its many other commercial uses, that made van Houten's inventions transformative. As one part of a battery of machines, the cacao press took its place in the steadily diffusing and rapidly standardizing process of chocolate manufacture.

At this point, late in the nineteenth century, chocolate took on the finished forms, either as solid bar or as covering for other confections, we know best today. The same is true

Conching machine, based on the 1876 invention by Rodolphe Lindt.

of the manufacturing processes that nearly all large-scale manufacturers follow to the present day. By the turn of the century, each step of the process was almost entirely mechanized. The first steps of chocolate manufacture are roughly the same as those that had always been used in preparing it: the beans are sorted and cleaned, and then put in large rotating roaster ovens that roast them slowly, both to develop the flavour and aroma and to make shelling easier. The roasted pieces are broken coarsely and hard bits of germimated bean and the pieces of shell are sieved and winnowed away respectively. The remaining beans, or nibs, are then ground more thoroughly. The friction of the grinding produces enough heat to melt the cocoa butter so that not a dry powder but rather a liquid paste, known as cocoa mass, is produced. It was essentially this mass, mixed with sugar and cooled again into a solid cake for making drinking chocolate, that was sold throughout the first half of the nineteenth century. In the modern process, the mass is then put into a press like that developed by van Houten, where the lemon-yellow cacao butter flows out. The resulting hard cake ('if one were banged on a man's head it would probably stun him' said a description from 1920) is then re-ground (and possibly 'Dutched') for processing into cocoa powder, or it is moved into chocolate production. For making chocolate, the pressed cake is recombined with sugar, traditionally in a *mélangeur* like that developed by Suchard in 1826, which is two heavy granite millstones which sit in a revolving granite basin. This sweetened mixture is then recombined with some cocoa butter or with other fats, vanilla, milk powder and whatever other ingredients are to be added and passed through a series of rollers which mill the particles into ever-finer granules. The only major innovation in the process that has happened since this era came after the Second World War with the addition of lecithin, an emulsifier made either from eggs or more often from soy. It is added both to cocoa and chocolate to improve blending and texture. The final step is conching, the process developed by Rodolphe Lindt. This process, which according to connoisseurs should take at least three days, often now takes place in hours. Finally, the chocolate, which up until this point has been kept at about 65–70°C, is moulded and tempered, that is, cooled quickly to about 40°C in order to force the cocoa butter to form crystal structures that will resist melting.

While chocolate took on its familiar forms just over a century ago, it was some time before these forms became widespread through all parts of society. It was not until nearly the turn of the century that a chocolate bar was affordable for the working classes in Belgium, for example. Cocoa, by contrast, became affordable and increasingly was seen as a nutritious foodstuff and meal replacement. As early as 1780 the British government had commissioned from the

American GIs in Normandy distributing chocolate to children, June 1944.

firm of J. S. Fry & Sons a standard ration of chocolate (in the form of solidified cocoa mass as described above) for seamen in the Royal Navy as a nutritious food source and alternative to rum. Fry's proudly referred to this naval connection in their advertising for many years. By the time of the First and Second World Wars, chocolate had completed its march to a mass-produced standard-issue foodstuff, and national firms proudly and patriotically (and of course lucratively) contributed it to the standard rations of the armed forces on all sides. Already in the First, but particularly during the Second World War, such chocolate rations were used symbolically to turn soldiers from all sides back into men when they encountered civilian populations, serving as paternal peace offerings to children and often more loaded gifts to women.

Cadbury's advertisement: solid chocolate as a treat for middle-class children.

'Whitening' Chocolate – Bourgeois Domestication

As we have seen, chocolate had been associated with women from the conquest of South America onwards, but in the early nineteenth century this association occurs in a new context. Far from the black magic wrought in the back streets of seventeenth-century South American cities, Victorian chocolate is linked to a thoroughly domestic idea of femininity primarily justified and fulfilled by motherhood. The ideology of the bourgeois family was central to nineteenth-century Europe, and chocolate, as ever, found its place at the era's heart. The new, and recognizably modern, advertisements of the Victorian era show how chocolate producers were able to exploit the simultaneous development of manufacturing processes, branding and the nuclear family.

Unlike the 'conversation pieces' of the eighteenth century, which show chocolate as an aristocratic accessory, nineteenth-

Fry's chocolate advertisement, 1920s.

century images of chocolate in the home are cosy and emphatically middle-class. Chocolate is not a luxury associated with sensual indulgence but healthy nourishment for growing families, what caring mothers provide for their children. The link between chocolate and childhood strengthened through

Chocolate as mother's milk: Helm cocoa advertisement, *c.* 1900.

the nineteenth century. Chocolate adverts from the middle of the century onwards were filled with pictures of frolicking, often chubby and cherub-faced children. The motif of happy families, with a direct appeal to mothers as the source of this happiness (as well as the supplier of cocoa), became an important component in marketing chocolate. In its new guise as nutritious food, chocolate adverts mustered images that were of maternal and/or nurturing femininity, as in Dutch manufacturer Droste's now-famous cocoa label featuring a nurse, introduced around the turn of the century.

The rise of the chocolate box in the same period provides some famous illustrations of this new identification with bourgeois domesticity. Like so many other developments in the creation of familiar forms of chocolate, the development of bite-sized filled chocolates arranged in a box that is at least as important to the purchase as the contents resulted from the combination of new technologies and broader social change. Cadbury's put the first box of chocolates on the market in 1868, shortly after importing their Van Houten press and increasing production. It was also in the 1860s that the first factory-produced greeting cards were sold, featuring similar images to those used to decorate the earliest chocolate boxes. The boxes were designed to outlast the contents and they were often used as long-term repositories for small objects of emotional value, particularly letters, as if the chocolates were both representing and marking the place of future tokens of love. It is easy to see how, in this context, the taste and ingredients of the chocolate could become secondary to the symbolism of the packaging, which, then as now, offered a simulacrum of the jewellery box to which it might be a forerunner. In the early years of the twentieth century and especially after the First World War, chocolate packaging proliferated. Decorated tins were cheaper to produce than decorated boxes, as well as being more durable. Tins of Quality Street, which are still a feature of a great many British Christmas gatherings, were first produced in 1936, with both the name and the figures on the tin taken from a typically nostalgic play by J. M. Barrie, the author of *Peter Pan.*

Britain was not the only place where the development of a manufacturing process for producing chocolate products went hand-in-hand with key packaging and marketing developments. In 1912 the Brussels chocolatier Jean Neuhaus (notably the grandson of a confectioner from Switzerland) developed a technique for making a hard chocolate shell for making filled chocolates or pralines. The name 'praline', referring to filled chocolates, sometimes generates confusion, particularly in the anglophone world. Especially in North America, the word also refers to a confection of nuts (normally pecans) and caramel, and is furthermore similar to the term 'praliné', which now refers to a specific type of nut and sugar (and sometimes chocolate) confection often used as a filling in chocolates. All of these words derive from the name of the seventeenth-century French Maréchal du Plessis-Praslin, whose cook purportedly invented the sugar-coated nuts. In a time of rapidly evolving confections and rising standards of living, the new filled chocolates rapidly caught on as a refined and elegant treat, and the word itself spread into German and Dutch as a synonym not for sugar and nuts but chocolate confections. Such filled chocolates soon spread beyond Neuhaus and became a trademark of Belgian confectionery more generally. The firms Leonidas (founded by a Greek-born American in 1910) and Godiva (established in 1926, now owned by a Turkish company) followed suit, also specializing in filled chocolates. Today, specialist manufacturers use the form to experiment with ever more exotic fillings and flavours such as black pepper and tamarind.

Godiva chocolates.

Unlike Cadbury's heavily decorated and reusable chocolate box, Neuhaus took a different tack in packaging their new creations. In 1915 Neuhaus's wife Louise Agostini, a ballerina by training, replaced the paper cones in which pralines were originally sold with a one-piece, hand-folded box, the *ballotin*. The *ballotin* was never patented and soon became, as it remains, a widely recognized sign of superior chocolates, which were particularly associated with Belgium partly because of the success of the Neuhaus firm. These elegant but flimsy cardboard boxes have promised high quality, 'hand made' chocolate for nearly a century, while hinged tins which last for decades are associated with inferior, mass-produced candy. For post-industrial consumers, elitism can be proved by a preference for form over function, but there is also a tendency to prize what is, or appears to be, artisanal and 'hand-crafted' over what is obviously the result of a mechanized process. Cheap chocolates which come in tins and bear the stamp of the machines that made them, perhaps in the form of animals or flowers, also come with descriptions which make no reference to the manufacturing process. Quality Streets include 'orange-flavoured truffle with orange crunchy pieces' and 'soft toffee finger dipped in milk chocolate', while even the newly repackaged Black Magic, intended to profit from a perceived vogue for the 'dark' chocolate which has always been a minority (and elite) taste in the UK, limits itself to 'dark chocolate wrapped around smooth praline with chopped roasted hazelnuts'. By contrast, Neuhaus's 'Caprice' 'harbours an incredibly crunchy nougatine. A subtle mix of caramelised sugar and hazelnuts that melts in the mouth, is folded and filled by hand before being immersed in a chocolate dip.' Montezuma's, an artisanal British chocolatier, assures buyers that, 'Each and every truffle is handmade

Origins are back: Montezuma chocolate bar.

by our skilled chocolatiers who pass all that pride and passion into great chocolate.' The more expensive and 'better' the chocolates, the more they have been handled, folded, immersed, filled and generally fondled. The cheap stuff pops unashamedly from a machine, like bullets.

These multiplying forms and packages for chocolate in the nineteenth century were associated with maternity, domesticity and romantic love – but only for the middle and upper classes. Discussion of chocolate became decidedly paternalistic when aimed at the working classes. Solid chocolates were treats for middle- and upper-class women and children, but for working-class families, cocoa became an equivalent to soup – warm, 'nourishing' and cheap. In discussions of chocolate's benefits to the working classes, its metaphorical and/or material association with milk – a pure and healthy substitute for solid food – gained new emphasis. Chocolate had long been drunk as a nourishing food substitute among the poorer classes in South America (and was a sanctioned way of 'cheating' on Catholic fast days among most classes), and as it became more affordable in Europe, such uses were similarly encouraged. Like sugar, which was similarly promoted to the working classes, chocolate appeared as abstract food – pure calories to fuel working bodies. Certainly the association of chocolate drinking with languor and idleness had vanished by the end of the nineteenth century. Instead, it was considered something that would boost industry and production. A 1906 treatise claimed: 'Cacao is the most nourishing of all drinks, it is almost without exception the cheapest food that we can put together. One could call it meat and drink. If only the poorly-nourished working man and the overworked factory child could be put in a position to use it instead of that brew they call coffee and tea, they would benefit from it in all respects.' Of

Cocoa as fuel for manly work: a Cadbury's advert from around 1900. Note the working-class habit of drinking from the saucer.

course the ruling classes would also benefit if workers would adopt this apparent miracle food to keep them working rather than demanding things like, say, increases in their material means or better conditions for children in factories.

Chocolate's stimulating properties, which the same book credited as greater than coffee's but less than tea's (!) were also mentioned in this regard. (This was measured by pure amounts of caffeine, teeine and theobromine, respectively, under the erroneous assumption that they all have the same effect.) Chocolate was not only thought of as a replacement for food, but particularly among the temperance-minded (who included the owners of a number of chocolate factories), it had long been seen as a wholesome replacement for drink. Not only would it keep the factories running, chocolate would thus also counteract the disorderly proclivities of the lower classes.

The identification of chocolate as fuel for 'manly' work contained another irony within the chocolate industry. While bourgeois women and children became the most visible consumers of chocolate, with increasing mechanization, and thus decreasing levels of heavy physical labour involved in processing, women and children also began to make up larger and larger proportions of the labour force manufacturing chocolate. By the turn of the century, the majority of those working in chocolate factories in France, Britain and Germany were women, and to a lesser extent children. A 1920 treatise describes how most of the steps in making chocolate cremes are undertaken by men, but assures readers that 'the covering of cremes and the packing of the finished chocolates into boxes are performed by girls. Covering is light work requiring a delicate touch, and if, as is usual, it is done in bright airy rooms, is a pleasant occupation.' The description of paid factory labour is made here to sound much more like the pastimes of more well-to-do women like needlework or other decorative hobbies, taking place in an aesthetically pleasing, almost domestic, environment. Many of the larger companies were well-known for their paternalistic care of their employees –

women employees of Cadbury's are apparently still issued a Bible and a red carnation upon their wedding day – though at least by the twentieth century, the need to employ married women remained a continual contradiction of the ideal of the domestic housewife that companies such as Rowntree's sought to promote externally.

Paternalistic contradictions aside, many nineteenth-century firms did indeed see their factories as places to improve manufacturing processes and products but also the lives of their workers as well. In Britain it is particularly noteworthy that all of the chocolate firms that grew to prominence in the nineteenth century were owned by Quakers. Fry's in Bristol, Cadbury's in Bournville (near Birmingham) and Rowntree's in York each owned model factories which supplied housing and access to education to many of their workers. In addition, many of them did work actively – if not always successfully

Women working in Rowntree's factory in York. Note the decor on the walls and efforts to make this a domestic atmosphere.

– to combat the slave trade. Of Mennonite rather than Quaker heritage, Milton Hershey perhaps took the role of philanthropic capitalist to its greatest extreme at his business in the 'Quaker State'. In the years after he bought the equipment from the Chicago Exposition, Hershey did not merely build a factory, but starting in 1903 he built the entire model town of Hershey, Pennsylvania, complete with houses on tree-lined streets, parks, schools, stores, banks and so on. The town continues to thrive, now not just as the home of Hershey manufacturing (which it still is), but also as a tourist attraction, supplemented by resorts and amusements that are all owned by the Hershey company.

As chocolate was adopted by more of the bourgeoisie in Europe, it was domesticated not only within the ideal nuclear family, but also within the other great social invention that came into its own in that century: the nation. The emphasis on domestic manufacturers of chocolate slowly came to obscure the places where the cacao was grown (though as we will see below, not entirely). Many of the advertisements for chocolate make the link between family and nation quite explicitly. On chocolate labels and adverts, chocolate factories proudly displayed themselves as part of national and urban landscapes, while images of frolicking children within them emphasized – sometimes simultaneously – the maternal nature of feminine homelands. In addition to these urban developments, nations like France that were beginning to record their various regional foods into a catalogue of rich and varied national traditions began to explore the artisanal roots of chocolate. The local cultures of chocolate in places like Bayonne were re-crafted into parts of national folklore, hallowing relatively recent customs with the incense of time-honoured tradition. Such images of 'natural' homelands were always misleading, however, particularly in the case of the two countries we now most associate with fine chocolate. Chocolate's associations with Switzerland and Belgium have nothing to do with any native natural product, nor did either have direct colonial cacao connections. For a number of reasons Switzerland happened to be a centre of industrial innovation. Belgians, on the other hand, showed themselves above all adept at creating and marketing filled chocolate confections.

Chocolate's association with milk of course strengthened its maternal connection with the nation. The best-known case in point is the association with Alpine landscapes and cows that came with the rise of Swiss chocolate manufacturing late in the nineteenth century. Though the expansion of Swiss chocolate was based on modern, technological processes, the images of unspoiled Alpine meadows embedded these products in supposedly ancient Swiss tradition. Such natural 'homeland' landscapes have long had feminine associations, but these were made explicit by the presence of milkmaids and placid cows. Similarly, a chocolate bar by the Belgian firm Callebaut from around the same time featured a 'typical' Low Countries milkmaid foregrounded on a scene of windmills and cows. These inward-turning visions of national landscapes nevertheless quickly became stereotypical marketing symbols. Peter's (the inventors of milk chocolate) marketed their product in America as 'high as the Alps in quality', with an advertisement showing an Alpine hiker. The ad praised the chocolate's 'absolute cleanliness' and also offered the illustrated booklet 'An Ascent of the Matterhorn' free with purchase. Eventually, any actual connection to Switzerland became superfluous. This can be seen most clearly in Swiss Miss, a brand of hot chocolate developed in America by a Sicilian family, which has been using the Alps and milkmaid theme to promote its 'European-style' chocolate since the 1950s.

The images of purity and health attached to chocolate were diminished somewhat by the rampant practices of adulteration that were common in the nineteenth-century food industry. Particularly after cocoa butter came into its own, this more expensive product was skimmed off and sold elsewhere, to be replaced in the final product by animal fats, oils or egg yolks, resulting in chocolate that went rancid quickly. Furthermore, a wider range of substances were added to create bulk and substance. Relatively harmless ingredients like potato starch, rice and pea flour and the husks of the cocoa beans were added, but less edible and downright toxic ingredients such as brick dust, red lead and vermilion also found their way into chocolate. In 1850 the British medical journal *The Lancet* began to test the purity of a range of newly industrialized products. Among the alarming discoveries was that just over half of their sample of chocolate contained red ochre from ground bricks.

The results of such revelations were, fortunately, laws outlawing such activities, most notably in Britain the Food and Drugs Act of 1860 and the Adulteration of Food Act in 1872. Over and above this, however, came an increased emphasis on 'purity' in chocolate. This was yet another way in which the focus on the manufacturer obscured the origin of the beans as the source of authenticity. While sources from early in the century emphasized the quality of 'pure' Caracas *criollo*, by the end of the century domestic manufacturers like Cadbury put themselves forward as symbols to vouch for the pure *chocolateness* of their products.

'Blackening' Chocolate – Race, Exoticism and Slavery

Chocolate's 'whitening' through associations with milk, childhood, national families and landscapes did not fully erase its 'colouring' as a colonial product: quite the contrary. Chocolate's spread and transformation in the North Atlantic world in the nineteenth century was accompanied by profound transformations in the economics of cacao cultivation. As cacao began to spread throughout the tropical colonial world in the late nineteenth and early twentieth centuries, chocolate's image, particularly in Europe, was also 'blackened' in a number of ways.

Particularly with the upheavals that were occurring in Latin American chocolate production, speculators looked for new places to grow cacao. Via imperial routes, cacao planting travelled to European holdings in Africa and particularly Dutch colonies in Indonesia. Almost from the very start of European exploration, plants began to circulate in what

There is a long history of child labour in cacao production. Youthful toilers on a lime and cocoa estate, Dominica.

would become the colonial world (Mexican cacao seedlings were apparently brought to Indonesia as early as 1515), but in the nineteenth century it began to happen systematically. The pioneers were the Portuguese, who, just before their colony of Brazil gained independence, took forastero cuttings to their colony on the island of São Tomé, off the coast of West Africa, in 1819. Over the course of the intervening decades, cacao spread first through the other Portuguese holdings, including the neighbouring island of Príncipe and the Spanish Fernando Pó (now Bioko), and then onto the mainland and thence into the British, French and German holdings beyond. The late nineteenth-century boom in European chocolate consumption and the European nations' 'scramble for Africa' were closely intertwined. In 1910, its peak year of production, tiny São Tomé was the largest single exporter of cacao in the world, to be decisively supplanted three years later by the booming British colony of the Gold Coast (now Ghana). These were literally the seeds for the present state of cacao production: particularly after disease destroyed vast numbers of cacao trees in Brazil in 1986. Top producer Côte d'Ivoire (which had no exports at all until 1904) and Ghana now account for 70 per cent of the world's cacao.

This shift in chocolate economics did not go unnoticed among chocolate consumers. As one aspect of its absorption into national fantasies, chocolate became a lens through which Europeans could view their empires. Late colonial powers Germany and Belgium in particular emphasized the blackness of chocolate. Chocolate-covered cream confections became known as *Negerküsse* ('negro kisses') (a term borrowed, incidentally, from the French) and *Mohrenköpfe* ('moor's heads'), names which they carried until quite recently in both Germany and the Netherlands. The German brand Sarotti is symbolized by the 'Sarotti Moor', which remains to this day one of

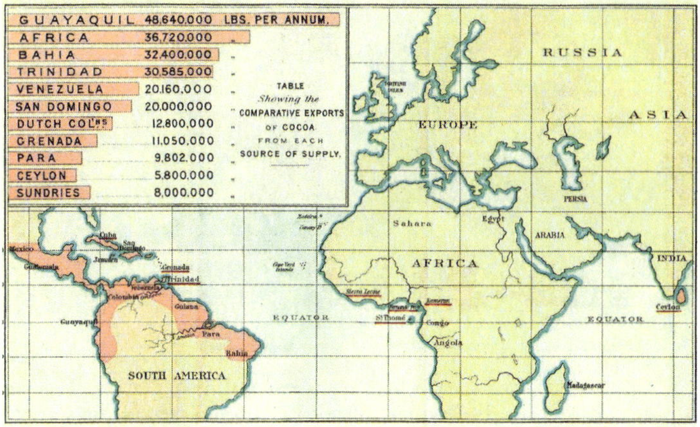

Map of the chocolate world, 1903. Ten years later, the bulk of production had moved to West Africa.

the most widely recognized brands in Germany. The figure, introduced in 1918 – not accidentally around the same time Germany lost its colonies – shows a black-skinned servant in Moorish robes. In earlier times the figure was also racially exaggerated with bulging eyes and large red lips. While the image made reference to the firm's first residence in Berlin's *Mohrenstrasse* (Moor street), its popularity had far more to do with Germany's colonial longings and fantasies. As an interesting footnote, the 'Moor' was transformed in 2004 into Sarotti's 'magician of the senses' – given lighter skin and had his serving tray replaced by 'magic' stars – replacing racial fantasies about servile Africans with equally racialized fantasies about the sensual and magic East. Similarly, the Belgian chocolate manufacturer Charles Neuhaus lent the name Côte d'Or to his new chocolate firm after returning from a trip to the African territory (Gold Coast) in 1883 to source cacao for it. The resulting label for Côte d'Or chocolate featured a mishmash of exotic symbols of Africa: an elephant, a pyramid and

The Sarotti Moor.

a palm tree, only the last of which in any likelihood was actually to be found in West Africa. The company (now a division of Kraft Foods) still proudly displays these symbols, particularly the elephant, now as evidence of the 'exotic experience' and, paradoxically, the enduring *tradition* of their chocolate.

While chocolate wrappers and advertisements associated the product to European consumers with fantasies of the exotic realms where cacao was cultivated, on occasions when the finished products arrived back in Africa (which is to this day relatively rare), they did so as the essence of metropolitan refinement and the civilizing influence of empire. A popular image from the German colonial adventure shows colonists making themselves 'at home' in Africa with well-known German products, notably Mumm sparkling wine and Stollwerck's chocolates. In a less optimistic mood, an advert for Fry's from around the turn of the twentieth century shows a crate of chocolate washed ashore on an African coast from a wrecked British ship (an ambiguous image at best, given Fry's association with the Royal Navy), surrounded by dark-skinned natives marvelling at the new product. At 'home' as well, chocolate showed Europeans the benevolence of empire. The popular chocolate-banana drink Banania in France is adver-

'Christmas in Cameroon': Chocolate returns to Africa as a luxury treat for German colonists, alongside German sparkling wine.

tised with a smiling Senegalese soldier exclaiming 'Y'a bon' ('that good') who at once embodies the 'black power' of chocolate and the benevolent, civilizing influence of empire.

Colonial fantasy was also repeatedly pierced by bitter reality. Slave labour, especially performed by Africans enslaved and transported across the Atlantic, had become a fundamental part of cacao cultivation over the course of the eighteenth century, particularly in the Caribbean and eastern side of South America. Opponents of the slave trade had long noted its connections with the chocolate industry, and Quaker industrialists such as Cadbury had long worked to eliminate it. Abolition was a long, slow, complicated process that continued throughout the century. While the slave trade was outlawed relatively early in the century, either *de jure* or *de facto* through British blockades and revolutionary strife, actual slavery was allowed to continue. Colombia ended slavery officially in 1851 and Venezuela (where, it will be recalled,

Chocolate goes back to Africa. A Fry's poster.

landowners had rebelled in part to keep their slaves) in 1854. The Portuguese did not outlaw it until 1875. In any event, as we shall see, the official abolition of slavery did not necessarily mean an end. Laws were often ignored or new, legalized systems of labour coercion were devised. As it was, enslaved labour continued to produce most of the cacao in Brazil into the 1880s, and it continued even later in West Africa. In many ways, slavery was not so much removed from the cacao trade but multiply re-*placed*. In one way, this is literally the case. As the transatlantic slave trade slowly dried up over the course of the century, territories in West Africa looked to find a replacement 'commodity' to export, and in-demand cacao was a more than likely candidate.

Along with cacao, the Portuguese had moved their system of forced labour plantations from Brazil to their colonies in West Africa. Once the slave trade had been officially abolished, it was no longer viable across the Atlantic, but at its source in West Africa it was still functional because it was internationally invisible. Scandal rocked the chocolate industry in Britain in the early 1900s after British journalist Henry Woodd Nevinson travelled in 1905 to Portuguese colonies in São Tomé and Angola to investigate rumours that practices of slavery still existed. Cadbury, who had long been buying cacao from São Tomé, had been investigating the rumours but when Nevinson's report – and photographs – were published first in *Harper's Monthly Magazine* and then in his book *A Modern Slavery*, the firm was openly accused of knowingly participating in slavery. Following a 1908 editorial in the London *Standard* that accused Cadbury's of hypocrisy for continuing to buy São Tomé cocoa, Cadbury Bros. sued for libel. In the ensuing trial, Cadbury argued that while it

Banania poster, 1915.

had been aware of labour abuses, its position as a purchaser of cocoa is what gave it any power at all to help improve conditions (lines of argument that would become familiar in arguments over divestment from South Africa much later in the century). The jury found in favour of Cadbury, but the publicity was far from all good, and the award of one farthing (a quarter of a penny) in damages hardly showed confidence in the firm's altruism.

What might be called a last, schizoid gasp of chocolate's long nineteenth century is visible in a Dutch ad campaign from 1958. The advert begins with the standard admonition to mothers to feed their children 'pure' and 'nutritious' chocolate: 'MOTHER, give them more than something tasty. Give them something nutritious at the same time . . . Venz chocolate sprinkles. Then they get pure chocolate – full of easily digestible fats, proteins and calcium.' Opposite the image of the product – complete with its picture of the happy child on the label – there is an image of Indonesian natives, gently and generously offering up their harvest of cacao pods. As usual, this advert covered up a more complex relationship. This vision of maternal/colonial benevolence came ironically – but probably not coincidentally – in the same year that the Indonesian government nationalized Dutch businesses and the Dutch were formally ejected from their former colony. As in so many other circumstances, chocolate was called in – symbolically at least – to smooth over and 'sweeten' bitter feelings.

4
The Chocolate Box

By the end of the Second World War, chocolate had acquired its familiar forms and most of its familiar associations. In the second half of the twentieth century chocolate has become ubiquitous in the Western world, an everyday purchase for millions of people. Particularly as firms try to come up with new ways of marketing this familiar product, the meanings and associations of chocolate have continued to twist and turn. While chocolate manufacture and consumption has spread globally, national styles and patterns of consumption have remained strong. The origins of chocolate, particularly its Latin American roots, which were first exoticized and then mostly erased over the course of the long nineteenth century, have returned on the tides of artisanal authenticity and concern over fair trading. To the extent it had ever disappeared, chocolate's image as a decadent indulgence has resurfaced – with both positive and negative connotations – particularly in its associations with women.

Economically speaking, the main development since the end of the war has been increased globalization and consolidation of the chocolate industry. Because of the climate conditions it favours, cacao is still restricted to the parts of the tropical zone to which it had spread in the nineteenth century.

The interruption of chocolate supply and demand caused by the Second World War was followed by the emergence of a larger global marketplace and increasingly powerful multinational firms that came to penetrate national markets. Four firms, Archer Daniels Midland, Cargill, Barry Callebaut and Nestlé, now handle over half of the world's cacao beans. Most of these cater to industry, and supply a large amount of chocolate *couverture*, which is melted and used as a component in making a wide range of chocolate confections. Furthermore, via mergers and acquisitions, most of the familiar firms that defined chocolate production and marketing 100 years ago are now brands or subsidiaries in major multinational corporations. US-based giant Kraft Foods, for example, now owns Suchard, Côte d'Or and Baker's, among many

Confectionery on display in a shop.

others. Beyond these major industrial suppliers who go largely unnoticed by consumers, certain individual chocolate products like Mars bars are recognized the world over (even though they actually vary in form from country to country). Ironically, what most Americans recognize as one of their most quintessential national products, the chocolate chip, is most commonly associated with the Swiss giant Nestlé.

The 'globalization' of chocolate is not always what it appears. Hershey's chocolate, which many Americans still view as standard, has a slightly sour flavour that has never caught on in most places outside the US. When Britain joined what was then the European Community in 1973, its chocolate with high milk and vegetable fat content did not meet the criteria to be sold as chocolate, and names such as 'household milk chocolate' (stressing, as ever, connections with milk and domesticity) or even 'vegelate' were mooted. The controversy over British chocolate was only resolved in 2003, when the EU ruled that other countries were not allowed to label British chocolate as 'chocolate substitute' due to its vegetable fat content. Beyond these regional differences, there are also large portions of the world where chocolate is not the ubiquitous flavour or form it is in the European and anglophone world. In Trinidad, once home to some of Cadbury's most important plantations, some natives still drink what they call 'cocoa tea': a drink made from chocolate press cake much like what was consumed throughout much of the nineteenth century. In Africa, where the majority of the world's cacao is now grown, chocolate is still not often consumed. The same is true of the Arab world, and of Asia generally. Japan is a notable exception to this, coming in well below northern European per capita consumption, but on a par with Spain and Portugal, which were once the centres of chocolate consumption in Europe.

It is also worth remembering that for much of the period after 1945, these 'global' trends in chocolate production applied mostly to countries west of the 'Iron Curtain', although this is not to say that the Eastern Bloc was without chocolate. Probably the most famous chocolate to be produced on the far side of the 'Iron Curtain' came from the Soviet Union's Red October factory, which until recently was in the heart of Moscow. Founded originally by a German confectioner in 1867, the factory was stopped by the revolution in 1918 and restarted under the name Red October. The company soon established a number of popular treats, with imagery not drawn so much from that of the socialist tradition of stylized workers and peasants, but (like a number of aspects of Soviet society) from the Russian national tradition. Popular Red October chocolates thus feature motifs such as playing bears, as well as the very popular bite-sized chocolate bar called Alyonka, presumably the name of the little girl on the label.

In other Soviet Bloc countries, similar native chocolate industries developed on the foundations of what had gone before. In East Germany, the centralized 'Sweets Combine' (and later the 'People's Own Enterprise Chocolate Factory Halloren') took over Germany's oldest chocolate factory (built in 1802) in Halle (not to be confused with the town of the same name in Belgium, which is home to Côte d'Or) and in 1952 introduced the Hallorenkugel, a fondant-filled bonbon, which soon became a much-desired luxury. Later on, the brand Zetti brought out a range of chocolates, including the Zetti Bambina, which was modelled on the milk-rich Kinder chocolate in the West. The more rurally oriented economy of Bulgaria developed its own native chocolate brand, the label of which, also following the long-established tradition in the industry, featured a photo of a cow in a meadow. In

Advert featuring nostalgic chocolate boxes from Russia's famed Red October factory.

the absence of a visible brand name, this, the only chocolate officially available, was simply known as 'cow chocolate'. Especially when it first came out, it was a rare treat. As was true of most aspects of the economies of scarcity in these countries, periodic shortages plagued chocolate production, and supply varied greatly. While during some periods in the post-war era, annual per capita chocolate consumption in the Soviet Union was around eight kilograms, immediately after the collapse, it had sunk to below one kilo. In the face of one such shortage, the East German government in 1974 lowered standards for cacao percentage in milk chocolate from 25 per cent to a mere seven per cent (and one will recall that Cadbury's twenty per cent already disqualified it from being labelled chocolate), falling back on tried and true fillers such as cheap fats and pea flour to compensate for more expensive ingredients. The more successful experiment was the Schlagersüsstafel, a bar that contained no chocolate whatsoever.

These products have not all disappeared. Quite the contrary; many former Communist countries have seen strong waves of nostalgia for the Communist era, or at least its consumer goods. Particularly given the very sudden flood of Western goods which quickly came to replace many the familiar products of everyday life, such consumer longings are understandable. These feelings, known in Germany as *Ostalgie* ('East-algia'), have revived the fortunes of many companies, which in many cases, now privatized, continue or have begun anew to produce the familiar tastes. In East Germany in particular, they form a sort of privileged knowledge and access to a world that West Germans do not share. Beyond that, the chocolates' association with childhood has allowed the familiar, and now more widely available, products to stand in as innocent memories of life in the authoritarian system. They offer a way of not dismissing outright what for many were important and formative years of their lives.

Lands of Chocolate: Roaming Fantasies and Bitter Realities

In a 1991 episode of *The Simpsons* entitled 'Burns Verkaufen der Kraftwerk' (sic), a German consortium takes over the nuclear power plant in Springfield and the new managers call Homer in to account for his (in)activity as the plant's safety superintendent. When Homer proposes improvements to the company snack machines rather than nuclear safety, the managers express their sympathy for Homer's concerns with a polite chuckle, telling him 'we are from ze land of chocolate'. Instead of moving him on to more important topics, however, this phrase instead sends Homer into a reverie about the land of chocolate. In fairytale town where everything is made out of chocolate, he imagines himself frolicking with hopping Easter bunnies and taking monster bites out of a lamppost, fire hydrant and even a passing chocolate dog. As the pinnacle of happiness in this paradise where all chocolate is free, Homer's unimaginative consumer imagination finally leads him to: a chocolate shop where everything is half-price.

As they regularly do, the Simpsons provide some of the more astute insights on contemporary society, and perhaps even more so than was intended. The cartoon Germans' identification of their native land as the 'land of chocolate' is a case in point. Few three-dimensional Germans would make the same claim – which is not to say that they would not find their native chocolate superior to most US brands. While Germany does indeed have a long-established native chocolate industry, Americans' associations of chocolate with Germany are mostly a case of mistaken identity. 'German chocolate' is actually a reference to 'German's Sweet Chocolate', a sweetened bulk chocolate invented by the Englishman Samuel German in 1852 and still produced by the US firm Baker's. The confusion arose when a recipe for a cake based around this chocolate and iced with coconut and pecan was mistakenly printed in a Dallas, Texas newspaper in 1957 as 'German chocolate cake'. The confection has had Teutonic associations in the US ever since, and 'German chocolate' now suggests a higher or richer quality of chocolate in common US parlance. The Alps-and-lederhosen imagery surrounding much Swiss chocolate, combined with Americans' stereotypically vague sense of geography, has done the rest.

Homer's fantasy land also does not come completely out of the blue. In keeping with his childlike character, it resembles candy land realms of children's literature, though without the darker edges that one finds in Roald Dahl's *Charlie and the Chocolate Factory* or in 'Hansel and Gretel'. But as manufacturers try to find new ways of marketing chocolate to adults, they also find increasing recourse to exotic, mythical utopias. When Nestlé produced its first white chocolate bar for the American market in the 1980s, its adverts invoked the pastel paradises of Maxfield Parrish, filled with mountains, pools and marble, all in delicate pale shades. Like Sarotti's new 'magician of the senses' described in the last chapter,

Still from *Charlie and the Chocolate Factory*, 2005.

Chocolate origins as tourist fantasy: Trinidad on a booklet cover issued by Cadbury's in 1927.

many of these exotic utopias build on the images of the tropical landscapes that have long been used to advertise chocolate. US viewers of Saturday morning TV cartoons might remember the Tusk, the chocolate elephant that advertised

Kellogg's Cocoa Krispies cereal in the 1970s and '80s, or any of a number of jungle-themed mascots for the cereal before or since (ironically, another elephant advertised the chocolatey cereal in Latin America later on). Côte d'Or's website currently features a television advert in which one zooms, as if in a helicopter, through a fantasy African landscape made entirely of chocolate. Elephants, dancing natives and long rivers of chocolate cross this chocolate savannah as 'native' drums beat in the background.

These frequent visions of exotic or mythical realms go strangely hand-in-hand with a greater awareness of the actual origins and history of chocolate. The websites of most chocolate manufacturers contain a short piece on 'the story of chocolate' which outlines basics about where chocolate was found as well as how it is manufactured. At the Côte d'Or factory in Halle, Belgium, for example, there opened in 1996 a 'chocolate temple' where visitors are led on a tour of a mock-up of a Toltec temple and Spanish galleon, as well as a chocolate factory from the early 1900s – oddly without 'stopping' in Africa, from where the bulk of the imagery, as well as the cacao, of the brand comes. While many of these stories speak of the exotic lands and ancient cultures of cacao production, they normally have very little to say about the lives and cultures of the people who produce cacao in the present. The New Zealand-based 'chocolate designers' Bloomsberry embrace this view of globalized geography in typically hip (and ultimately cynical) terms. They announce cheerily that '[L]ucky for us, the cacao tree only grows in very hot tropical climates where it is consistently warm and very humid (and with great beaches)' but describe harvesting as 'very hot, dusty physical work that unfortunately we were unable to assist with as we were urgently summoned back to our air-conditioned head office for an important meeting'. It is thus perhaps no surprise that their '100% Guilt-free' brand chocolate bar cites everything from its recycled paper wrapper to a lack of animal testing, but has nothing to say about conditions of cacao workers.

This renewed emphasis on the cacao source, however partial, has by no means eliminated national associations of chocolate. The global expansion of chocolate trade has made certain national associations, most notably Switzerland,

Chocolate as fantasy world: 'Chocolate temple' from a German treatise in practical (!) confectionery-making.

Patrick Roger, *Harold*, sculpture in chocolate of a black planter.

Belgium and France, into important parts of chocolate's branding. Now more than ever, food products including chocolate need to be identifiably *from somewhere* – whether that somewhere is fact or fiction. Thus the US foods giant ConAgra Foods has recently intensified the 'Swiss-ness' in the packaging of its Swiss Miss brand (which, it will be recalled, was a brand started by an Italian-American in the US) with deeper colours and an emphasized Alpine landscape on its packaging.

As chocolatiers make their way through global commerce channels, 'local' products also begin to enter new hybrid contexts. Again, geographical fantasies play an important part. Recently, a Dutch franchise has begun marketing ice-cream and chocolates under the improbable sounding name of Australian. While the firm has no actual connection with Australia whatsoever, their chocolates are stencilled with vaguely 'Aboriginal' designs. In 2003 this drew sharp protest from the Aboriginal and Torres Strait Islander Commission, who felt that the company's use of such symbolism amounted to cultural theft of their sacred symbols. The Australian company argued that the designs were not Aboriginal symbols, but rather made by a Dutch artist 'inspired by' Aboriginal art. Nevertheless, the firm agreed in the end to help support the Aboriginal communities, and thus, at last, a link with the place was formed in retrospect. Ironically, this was around the same time that northern Australia actually was developing its own local cacao cultivation and chocolate production.

The lands associated with cacao growing have also come further into popular consciousness of chocolate with the increasing scrutiny on global trade inequality. Fairly traded chocolate is one of the fastest-growing segments of the current chocolate market. The move towards fairly-traded chocolate has long been associated with the more expensive, though not highest, end of chocolate. Fair trading's emphasis

The black and white worlds of chocolate: dark, single-origin chocolates next to white chocolates with national scenes.

on transparent sourcing and direct dealings with local growers certainly go hand-in-hand with the notions of purity and authenticity of origin that accompany most high-status foods. Such associations have proven a very effective means of establishing a solid and growing market niche for fairly traded chocolate among aficionados of high grade chocolate. The expansion of this niche has contributed to improving the situation and well-being of growers. At the same time, however, there is no *natural* relation between fair trading and fancy chocolate. One could just as easily use fairly-traded cacao to make Kit Kats or Tootsie Rolls as single-source grand cru, though the fact that the former are not high-status foods means that people would be unlikely to pay the additional amount of money that using fairly-traded cacao would demand. On the higher end, the increased concerns with origins are a double-edged sword for improving conditions in the industry. While they increase consciousness of where chocolate is grown, and several high-end manufacturers such as Amadei have made important efforts towards fair trading, the labelling and discussion surrounding the origins of 'good chocolate' often obscure rather than highlight the trade and labour conditions of production.

Besides fair trading, more serious issues with chocolate's origins have begun to surface. Like their predecessors of 100 years before, recent journalistic investigations have revealed that slave and child labour is still alive in the cacao industry, particularly in West Africa. In 2001 two US congressmen sought to address this issue by working with chocolate firms to establish a 'slave-free' certification for chocolate. The Harkin-Engel Protocol, as it is called, set a target date of 1 July 2005 for industry to 'develop and implement credible, mutually-acceptable, voluntary industry-wide standards of public certification . . . that cocoa beans and their derivative product have been grown and/or processed without any of the worst forms of child labour.' Shortly after the protocol was introduced, Dutch TV journalist Teun van de Keuken began researching the sourcing of chocolate for a consumer investigative programme, and attempting to find out from various major chocolate firms if they could guarantee that their chocolate was not produced by forced labour. This proved impossible. Noting that according to Dutch law, any form of participation in the slave trade, including purchasing its products, is punishable, van de Keuken bought a candy bar and walked to the next police station to turn himself in. What followed was a lengthy effort to gather evidence and witnesses to have himself prosecuted, so that Dutch authorities would be forced to take action more generally on the issue, and at that point, he began to raise awareness worldwide. In July 2005 the chocolate industry failed to meet the goals of the Harkin-Engel Protocol (and at the time of writing has still not done so), and three major firms, Cargill, Nestlé and Archer Daniels Midland, were sued by the International

Labour Rights Forum. In a more personal response to the failure, Van de Keuken founded his own brand of chocolate, Tony's Chocolonely, which proudly bears a 'slave-free' emblem on the label. While it is the only chocolate bar aimed specifically at raising awareness of coerced labour, Tony's is not the only slave-free chocolate. According to most sources, the 'fair trade' certification on a bar of chocolate is a good indication of humane labour practices in addition to the prices that growers receive from manufacturers. In addition, cacao not from West Africa, while it may not be fairly traded, will probably not have involved coerced labour.

'Good Chocolate' vs 'Bad Chocolate'

Besides providing insights into the (mistaken) mental geographies of chocolate, Homer Simpson's romp through the 'land of chocolate' also portrays quite astutely the enduring polarity of chocolate as most of us encounter it in daily life: as a ubiquitous flavour that makes up an uneventful part of our food landscape, and as an expensive, exotic commodity sold in specialty shops. If anything, this polarity has become more entrenched in recent years, as manufacturers at a range of scales attempt to diversify and sell to more and more specialized consumers. However, as in Homer's fantasy, the meanings surrounding these two different versions of chocolate intermingle more often than most stories about chocolate would have one believe.

Beginning in the mid-1980s, a number of high-end chocolatiers, with French firms Valrhona and Bonnat at the forefront, set out to re-work chocolate as a gourmet food for the luxury market. Since then, new forms of chocolate lore have entered into popular knowledge and new criteria for determining the difference between 'good' and 'bad' chocolate have been established. Consciously modelled on the culture of wine-growing and tasting, chocolate joined a number of other foods, including coffee, olive oil, bourbon and beer, all of which have undergone similar revolutions in recent years. The new wisdom emphasizes a wide range of different flavours discernable in chocolate, knowledge of the unique characteristics of a number of species and growing regions for cacao, and above all a devotion to the chocolate in its purest form (along specific definitions of purity, which are central). This lore is laid out in relatively compact form in Chloé Doutre-Roussel's 2005 book *The Chocolate Connoisseur*. In it, she provides readers with a wide range of knowledge (including the 'taste map' of the tongue, which was debunked by physiologists 30 years ago) to guide them through this 'chocolate revolution'.

In exploring the lore, one learns that 'good chocolate' is dark, serious, rooted, pure, authentic, rare, artisanal, expensive, generally Catholic European (French and Italian), and healthy. In the realm of fine chocolate, the emphasis on chocolate's origins is driven by ideas of *terroir* adopted from viniculture. This is a trend that began in the mid-1980s with Bonnat's single-estate bars and came into its own in the mid-1990s with bars like Lindt's single country-of-origin chocolates and single plantation bars by a number of French firms. Much as chocolate connoisseurs in the 1700s insisted on high-quality Caracas *criollo*, connoisseurs of fine chocolate now distinguish between the flavours of cacao from Venezuela and Ecuador, but also Madagascar and Java, and individual plantations, such as Venezuela's fabled Chuao plantation. These bars are known as grand cru (a term that not only embraces places, but also vintage year). As the Italian gourmet chocolatiers Amedei (who now own exclusive right to the Chuao plantation) describe their line:

Amedei's single-estate *grand cru* bar from Venezuela's famed Chuao estate.

The Cru originate from individual production areas and, just as the grapes that flourish under a particular sun and from a specific soil, they have a marked personality and a decisive flavour. They are the most immediate and 'savage' expression of cacao. The individual plantations of origin interpret the genetic diversity of the cacaos existing today, from the beans which best highlight the characteristics of each plant type, selected, cultivated and processed in accordance with strict discipline in the countries of origin.

These ideas of genetic and local particularity spill over into more romantic and touristic visions of chocolate as the essence of 'savage' realms. Elsewhere Alessio Tessieri of Amedei writes: 'I feel the greatest, most beautiful sensations when I discover a virgin plantation, never visited by any westerner: I immediately think of how to transform it into a taste or an emotion to bring the perfume, and the atmosphere of that land to whomever tastes the chocolate.'

Producers of organic chocolates like the pioneering firm Green & Black's have also long sought to label the origins of their chocolate as a means of transparency as well as to capture such ideas of terroir and tradition. Even the US giant Hershey has recently joined the new fashion for organic, single-source chocolate with its 'Cacao reserve' line. Following the labelling conventions of high-end chocolate, labels for new line, laid out in 'portrait' not 'landscape' format, list prominently the location and cocoa percentage (although among true connoisseurs, this latter knowledge is now peripheral). In contrast to these various single-source chocolates, the products of West Africa are generally considered poorer quality. Apart from its abundance in the global market, which seldom boosts the status of any food, the fact that West African cacao is more or less exclusively of the forastero variety is the main reason why some experts consider the region a black hole of taste. With that said, however, Bonnat features a Grand Cru from Ivory Coast, and Amedei offers a Grand Cru (albeit from Ecuador) that offers 'a very rare example of "forester" of great aromatic impact and power'.

Much talk of purity and authenticity is also centred around getting closer to the essence of the bean. One expression of this has been quite literal: several manufacturers now offer bars that contain bits of cocoa nib, so that if one tastes carefully, one can taste the unrefined product. This has also meant attempting to revive the once moribund varieties of *criollo* and *trinitario* chocolate, particularly in the Americas, but also in Madagascar. The relatively isolated Chuao plantation in Venezuela has become particularly well-known for its historic and apparently 'pure' beans. Nowhere is bean lore more obsessive, however, than when dealing with the 'porcelana', a rare white *criollo* found in Venezuela. As Amedei enthuse: 'Porcelana is a cacao "criollo". It means genetically pure. It is the "father" of all cocoa.' Though almost certainly not intended, there are disturbing overtones in the discussions of the 'genetic purity' of this 'white' *criollo* – a term itself derived from notions of 'pure white blood' in people. Valrhona also wax rhapsodic about the white bean in describing their Porcelana del Pedregal, which is not a bar but a flower-shaped chocolate made from it:

> To fully express the flavours . . . it was necessary to associate them with a new shape and a new image. A fleeting sensation, but visible for the eye and discernible to the touch, a fragile ephemeral form reminding us that only one in a thousand flowers survives from the mass of blossom springing from the very trunk of the Porcelana trees; its frail petals are offered as a token of its authentic story.

Good chocolate is all about the authentic story. History plays an important role here, too, and like the mass manufacturers, most artisanal producers are keen to tell customers the history of their product. Unlike the histories of chocolate told by the major manufacturers, which are about discovery, innovation and corporate expansion (in short: *success*), the chocolate histories from connoisseurs are tales of preservation, rescue and redemption. Some of this focuses on the bean and the 'essence' of chocolate, which appear as things that were lost through years of mass manufacture and are now being restored to their original essence, flavour and native meaning. Some is to do with the craft of chocolate-making itself. Bonnat points to its artisanal tradition as 'handed down from father to son', while Doutre-Roussel points to the revival of older techniques and machinery in a lot of gourmet chocolate-making as essential to finding the essence of the chocolate. She argues that 'using old machinery, a producer is more likely to treat the beans with the respect they deserve, coaxing as much flavour out of them as possible, allowing them some individuality in their texture.' For all that they are new products, the message seems to be that they are actually *older*, more original, than their mass-produced counterparts.

'Bad' chocolate, in contrast, is everything that good chocolate is not: sweet, light, impure, placeless, mass-produced, cheap, fattening, addictive. It is a *cheap imitation* of good chocolate, never mind the fact that 'bad' chocolate has been around longer. Whilst stressing the importance of developing one's own 'chocolate profile' derived from an exploration of one's own tastes, Doutre-Roussel spends most of her book telling readers what they should *not* like. She is also quite clear about where the blame for the persistence of poor-quality chocolate lies. 'If customers enjoy and keep on buying chocolate that I would consider to be of inferior quality, then there is little incentive for the melters of couverture to invest in a more expensive chocolate.' She is also careful, however, to help readers avoid the ultimate bourgeois sin of confusing price with quality. Good chocolate is expensive, but not all expensive chocolate is good. Just like in Brillat-Savarin's discussions of chocolate from nearly 200 years before, what is necessary on the part of the 'good' consumer of chocolate (who is of course ideally the consumer of 'good' chocolate) is the mental discipline of amassing the skills and knowledge to appreciate it, as well as the bodily discipline of not over-indulging. The 'good' consumer of chocolate is *passionate*: driven by an intellectual and spiritual quest for purity, novelty and innovation. The 'bad' consumer is *addicted*: driven by bodily urges or cravings and, in reacting to these, seduced by manufacturers into accepting something that is *not really chocolate*.

Current health wisdom has underlined differences between good and bad chocolate. As chemists and nutritionists try to get behind the complex make-up of chocolate, 'the darker the better' is the growing consensus: cacao's nutritious essence, as opposed to chocolate's thick bulky substance, becomes the key factor in determining what is healthy about it. For several years now, chocolate's mineral content has been believed to be beneficial to women. In her 1995 book *Why Women Need Chocolate*, nutritionist Debra Waterhouse argues that women crave chocolate in response to a genuine bodily need for these minerals. At the same time, however, the author also stresses that proper exercise and bodily discipline will also reduce cravings for the bad things in chocolate. The current interest in the health benefits of antioxidants has also fuelled chocolate's rehabilitation as a healthy food. These substances, which have been highlighted for their ability to help prevent cell damage, are found in green tea, red wine and above all in dark chocolate. Côte d'Or now features a separate section of their website devoted to antioxidants, as well as an 86 per cent bar specifically marketed to meet the need. Besides these health benefits, wisdom regarding chocolate's various ill effects is also changing. In the same breath as they debunk the myth of chocolate's aphrodisiac qualities, good chocolate proponents are also keen to point out that other deleterious effects of chocolate, such as its fattening and addictive properties, are not really due to the substance itself, but to its various additives. As Doutre-Roussel puts the matter succinctly: 'sugar is the evil in chocolate'. This 'evil' is necessary to keep the chocolate from being inedible, to be sure, and, as we shall see, 'evil' seems to be a necessary ingredient in enjoying chocolate for many people as well.

Besides embracing the antioxidants in 'good' chocolate, manufacturers are seeking to help combat the effects of 'bad' chocolate, while of course still selling it. Firms in Britain, most notably Cadbury Schweppes and Mars, launched in 2006 the 'Be Treatwise' campaign (www.betreatwise.org.uk). The campaign involves placing a 'Be Treatwise' reminder on the front of packets, and basic nutrition information on the

Apparently, only women need to worry about overindulging in chocolate: a recent ad campaign in Britain.

back, including recommended daily amounts and suggesting daily exercise to compensate for treats. It is worth noting that judging from its imagery and layout, the campaign is aimed largely at women, both as primary consumers and as those making nutritional choices for children. They seem to be the ones judged most likely to stray from the path of righteousness when it comes to chocolate. Again, as we shall see, this is also part of what chocolate seems to be about.

Women, Indulgence and Sex: Beyond Good and Evil?

Friedrich Nietzsche famously pointed to the distinction to be made between the different opposites of 'good', 'bad' and 'evil'. While 'bad' is an aesthetic value denoting ugliness or poor quality, 'evil' is a moral value. He argues that upon closer inspection, what we call 'evil' is often aesthetically good precisely because it is able heroically to break through the bounds that morality places on beauty. Much of the lore surrounding high-end chocolate equates the aesthetic goodness of 'real' chocolate with certain notions of moral goodness based around purity and discipline. While it pleases the senses, 'good' chocolate does not make you crave sex or get fat or do anything else that would imply losing control of your body. Most popular discussions of chocolate do not compete for this moral high ground, however. Instead, chocolates across the board tend to invoke the 'evil' nature of chocolate as its best quality. Perhaps ironically, given Nietzsche's reputation as a misogynist, this applies particularly to the way chocolate is marketed to women.

Ideas of chocolate as a dark, seductive power are of course long-standing, and have been through a number of transformations. Rowntree's Black Magic chocolates, which first appeared in 1933, invoked this dark power explicitly. Advertising from the 1930s through the 1950s sold the chocolates as an exquisite treat well-suited for men to use in wooing upper-class women. Such upper-class fantasies generated by a relatively inexpensive product of course also spoke to the class and economic uncertainties of their era. But while some of the 'dark power' was clearly class and money, sex was also a key implication and desired outcome. In one advert from 1934, a woman writes of the chocolates she has received from her beau: 'We silly creatures are always so thrilled when a man thinks us worth the very best. Imagine it, a big box of these new Black Magic chocolates on my dressing table. My dear, each choc's an orgy!'

In more recent years, chocolate advertising has eliminated the middleman, as it were, and marketed chocolate directly to women for their own pleasure. A recent trade publication argues that specialized addresses to women (alongside fair trading) represent one of the fastest-growing trends in chocolate marketing. Rebranding chocolate as healthy and not incompatible with keeping one's figure is one element of this. But another side is also clearly visible. Indulgence in chocolate is portrayed as a means of liberation and self-satisfaction. Women who buy chocolate for themselves, it would seem, have moved beyond good and evil. The US firm Seattle Chocolates has recently produced a new line of 'Chick Chocolates' aimed at women who pursue their own pleasure. According to the firm, these chocolates 'satisfy a woman's intense sweet craving while providing a good giggle. In a stylish box reminiscent of cosmetic packaging, Chick is portable and portion-controlled, with three individually

Fantasies of upper-class romance: Rowntree's Black Magic chocolates advert from 1937.

wrapped pieces in each box.' Presumably this 'portion control' is what leaves women free to eat such chocolates 'not slowly, but all by yourself, selfishly, because you'd be crazy not to'. Chocolate designers Bloomsberry have also embraced feminine self-indulgence as a key sales line. Their packaging designs dress up chocolate bars (all of which are actually the same variety of either milk or dark chocolate) to resemble other women's products, such as Beauty Bar, which looks like a fancy soap wrapper, or Girth Control ('Helps you avoid "thinking about it" for 15 minutes'), which resembles a pharmaceutical box. Women's sense of power is appealed to

After Eight chocolates advertisement.

through bars that label chocolate as Broomstick Fuel (referring to witches, not household chores) or, more traditionally, through the Marital Bliss bar, with a decidedly skewed '50–50' apportion of the chocolate into 'his' and 'hers'.

One of the most common motifs in chocolate advertisement is the woman on the sofa, enjoying the solitary pleasure of chocolate, such as in a recent ad by Côte d'Or. The woman lies supine on the couch, sharing neither couch nor chocolate nor fantasy, her book draped below waist level to suggest which part of her it appeals to, where the shadow of the Côte d'Or elephant also falls. In some ways, these women can be read as direct descendents of the women portrayed in the eighteenth century, languidly sipping chocolate in their boudoirs while consuming similarly questionable fiction. Unlike her counterpart of three centuries ago, for whom chocolate was evidence of a general state of luxury, the present-day woman on the sofa seems to be transforming her domestic surroundings into something luxurious and decadent, and/or escaping from them entirely by eating chocolate. Worryingly, a woman being idle in the domestic sphere still seems vaguely decadent. Over and above this, however, it is notable how ideas of 'good' chocolate's 'darkness', luxury and exoticism are still present here. The difference is that here it is a bodily indulgence, something that satisfies a bodily urge rather than an aesthetic quest.

Because chocolate often represents women's sexuality, it also appears in popular culture as a replacement for sex. Thanks to the wonder of the internet, and friends who forward such messages, most of us are by now probably familiar with at least ten reasons why chocolate is better than men, or better than sex (they seem to amount to roughly the same thing). Most of the reasons have little to do with any quality of chocolate beyond the fact that it tastes good and is inanimate, thus lacking any will or desire of its own. Essentially, such lists trot out a series of clichés about the relative amounts of pleasure men and women experience in heterosexual sex. Chocolate rates in particular as a superior oral pleasure. In seeming confirmation of these pieces of folk wisdom, a 2007 study – sponsored by food manufacturers and using a new

Return of the Catholic connection? *Chocolat*, 2000.

brand of dark chocolate as test object – found that chocolate was more physically stimulating than kissing one's partner passionately. Without dismissing the scientific value of the results (though it is questionable which science is their main beneficiary), the fact that the study was conducted at all says much about the place of chocolate in our lives and how we relate it to sex and bodily pleasure.

Popular portrayals of chocolate consumption are not merely about liberation and women taking charge of their own pleasure, but also quite clearly about transgressive, *sinful* pleasures. Writing and adverts for chocolate are filled with words such as 'sin', 'temptation' and 'wickedness'. In this regard, it seems that chocolate's associations with Catholicism have returned in full force, but with new meaning, as in the French Suchard ad that stated simply: 'It is a test sent to us by the Lord.' The recent film *Chocolat*, based on the novel of the same name by Joanne Harris, also brings chocolate and Catholicism into the same frame, but as polar opposites rather than the close associates they had been in past times. In the film, chocolate does not appear as part of the cycle of sin, confession and reconciliation (and renewed sinning), but instead the church attempts to stamp out chocolate altogether as a sensual pleasure – an attitude largely associated in our world with Protestantism. Most blatant is ice cream manufacturer Wall's '7 Deadly Sins' line of Magnum ice cream bars, which are, again, marketed entirely to women. Besides 'lust', which is made up of pink 'strawberry flavoured chocolate', the fold also includes a dark chocolate 'gluttony' and a predictably green (pistachio) 'jealousy'. But in the adverts for the Magnum bars, as in much chocolate advertising, the idea is not so much that sex is sin, but more generally that sinning is sexy. The 'sin', to the extent it is identified at all, is indulging in a sensual pleasure that might make one fat – though one would never know it from the women in the adverts. In this light, the 'Be Treatwise' campaign's suggested 30 minutes of exercise per treat also smacks distinctly of doing penance.

It must be said that for all they talk about sex, sin and exoticism, adverts for chocolate are ultimately tame in their suggestions. Quite apart from the fact that they sell a 'forbidden fruit' that is available cheaply anywhere, they are generally 'vanilla' in their sexual flavourings, and if anything seem to be struggling to keep up with even the mainstream values and experiences of chocolate consumers. Given the generally widespread visibility of gay characters in popular culture, for example, they do not seem to register on the chocolate horizon (an exception is the Magic Fairy bar – 'one poof and it's all gone' – by Bloomsberry). Chocolate instead appears as a way of practicing safe sin. Especially with their emphasis on chocolate as an escapist pleasure, the message of a number of chocolate adverts seems to be that in every woman beats the heart of Emma Bovary, but that Rodolphe Lindt's creation is a safer (and profitable) stand-in for any would-be Rodolphe.

Marketing chocolate to men: Nestlé's (formerly Rowntree's) Yorkie bar.

While chocolate is increasingly marketed to women as satisfying sensual or sexual appetites, to men it is still marketed mainly as it was in adverts for cocoa in the nineteenth century, satisfying a simple bodily appetite: a 'manly' hunger for food. Rowntree's (and now Nestlé's) Yorkie bar is the iconic case in point. Since its appearance in 1976, the bar has always been marketed to men, until recently drawing on US Marlboro-man type images of rugged and independent masculinity, such as truck drivers. Real men do not eat chocolate on sofas (and we darkly suspect that men who nibble it whilst writing cultural history books at their computers are barred from the club as well). In the 1990s, this acquired a more tongue-in-cheek aspect in adverts about an escaped convict, who was considered especially resourceful and dangerous because he had a Yorkie bar. Eating a Yorkie bar had become a manly act in itself. In 2001 Yorkie adverts finally cut to the chase with the slogan 'It's not for girls.' Besides the humour in Yorkie's embrace of the schoolyard-style claim – which Nestlé's website assures us 'resonates with today's British male' – the campaign claims to address men's sense of marginalization. 'In today's society, there aren't many things that a man can look at and say that's for him.' Those watching adverts during sporting events, of which Yorkie sponsors a number, might be baffled at this claim, but the main thrust of the adverts is the bar's power as a 'hunger buster'. Ironically, it is in selling chocolate to men, not to women, that size matters: 'With five solid chunks of chocolate, it's a man-sized eat!' In the land of chocolate, only women get fat: men just get hungry.

Notably, in the Western world, advertising visions of chocolate as sexual indulgence are directed almost exclusively at white women. Given the enduring and often overt racial overtones of chocolate, the implied 'sin' in a number of adverts is miscegenation. Chocolate is often presented to women in adverts by dark-skinned men in 'native' clothes, suggesting at once subservience and invoking ideas of 'native' sexual prowess. Similarly, when black women appear associated with chocolate, they are normally not the consumer but the (sexually) consumed. In 1996 Suchard chocolates produced an advertisement in France that showed a black woman, Tyra Banks (who made headlines most recently with an on-air feminist rant about women's body image), dressed only in small pieces of gold foil that look like the remnants of a chocolate wrapper and that also enhance the 'exotic' image by resembling tiger stripes. The caption of the advert read, 'Even though you said no, we heard yes.' While French adverts normally feature more nude female flesh and overt references to sex than those in the US or Britain, the clear reference to rape in the advert crossed a line. After a vigorous protest from women's groups, the designer apologised and the advert was withdrawn. Significantly, the racial element of the advert received little or no mention within the ensuing controversy.

Another ambiguous confrontation with the 'chocolate as black woman' theme came on Dutch television following the announcement in 2006 that the manufacturer of chocolate marshmallow confections known as 'Negro kisses' were changing the name to 'kisses'. Much of the public discussion around the change was about whether it was a matter of political correctness gone mad, and many who had grown up with the confection made no conscious connection between the sweet treats of their childhoods and disparaging racial images. The night the story made the television news, the newsreader Aldith Hunkar, who is of Afro-Caribbean origin, changed her regular sign-off. After she had wrapped up with most of the standard phrases, she paused, a mischievous smile spread over her face and she said, 'and the last negro kiss you get from me' and aimed a kiss at the camera. Judging from the discussion that ensued, anti-PC audiences saw this as evidence that she was on their side, and that her presence as a successfully integrated part of Dutch society was proof that the racial prejudice and inequality suggested by the name had long since disappeared. The shock it caused, however, with its reminder that the term still invokes images that apply to real people, made the light-hearted gesture seem far more ambiguous.

That ambiguity, or rather series of ambiguities, offers as good a summation as any of the current place of chocolate in our lives and indeed throughout much of its history. It remains a puzzling mixture between familiar and exotic, global and local, guilty pleasure and overlooked injustice. Its various stories disappear and reappear in sometimes unexpected times and ways. In describing their work as the ongoing construction of an idea and a myth, chocolatiers Amadei have come closest, and perhaps closer than intended, to capturing the various things chocolate means: 'The chocolate is an idea in which white and black blend; the pleasure and the transgression blend in lines and curves. We follow the emotions that transform the chocolate into the most precious myth, one which holds together childhood memories and the satisfaction of senses.'

Recipes

Chocolate and Lavender Cream

This is chocolate at its most deracinated. The use of herbs in sweet foods is an English habit going back to the Middle Ages, although perhaps also borrowed from the Middle East, and lavender has recently returned to fashion in food as well as perfume. All the ingredients except the chocolate are foreign to the New World. (Some consequences of globalization are to be celebrated.)

Serves 8

250 g (8 oz) granulated sugar
250 g (8 fl oz) white wine
juice of ½ lemon
600 ml (1 pint) double cream
1 or 2 lavender stems, with flowers
165 g (5½ oz) good plain chocolate, grated

Mix the sugar, wine and lemon juice in a heavy-based pan. Heat gently until the sugar dissolves, stirring occasionally. Stir in the cream and cook over a gentle heat, stirring constantly, until the mixture thickens. Add the lavender and the grated chocolate, and stir until the chocolate dissolves. Bring to the boil and then simmer the mixture for twenty minutes, or until dark and thick. Remove the lavender stems.

Cool, then pour into eight or more ramekins or small glasses. Cover the top with cling film and refrigerate (they keep well for 3–4 days). Decorate with a sprig of lavender.

Cowboy Cookies

Chocolate chip cookies have become synonymous with America, though as with so many national traditions, they are a relatively recent invention. The first ones, and the product they now contain, were famously developed in the 1930s by Ruth Wakefield of the Toll House Inn in Massachusetts in partnership with Nestlé. In spite of their novelty, their connection with the Inn spoke of quaint, colonial New England tradition.

The following recipe, the 'Cowboy Cookie', shows a further adaptation of the chocolate chip cookie into US national fantasy, with the addition of oatmeal somehow adding connotations of frontier life. They have been the Badenoch family recipe since grandmother Edith Badenoch spotted it in a women's magazine in the late 1940s. It is an economical recipe very much of its time – it's hard to imagine a recipe these days leading off with shortening. The 'cowboy' moniker also proved useful in persuading children who were sceptical about having their cookie recipe stretched with oatmeal.

1 cup (190 g) shortening
1 cup (180 g) brown sugar
1 cup (200 g) white sugar
2 eggs
¼ tsp baking powder
½ tsp salt
½ tsp baking soda
2 cups (240 g) flour
1 cup (180 g) chocolate chips
1 tsp vanilla
2 cups (180 g) oatmeal

Cream the shortening, brown sugar, white sugar and eggs until smooth, then mix in baking powder, salt, baking soda and vanilla. Add flour a little at a time, then stir in chocolate chips and oatmeal. Bake at 325° C for 12–15 minutes or until done.

'Historic' Hot Chocolate

This is a melange, an invention using modern ingredients in vague homage to the irrecoverable tastes of the seventeenth and eighteenth centuries. It is not 'Aztec', because we assume you do not have access to unrefined cacao or South American flora, and we assume that you prefer your chocolate sweetened. It might be rather like the beverage drunk at the Austens' wedding breakfast.

water and/or milk
approx. 30 g unsweetened chocolate per person (or, since you will be adding sugar anyway, your preferred chocolate)
grated sugar
cinnamon bark, vanilla, ginger and/or (inauthentically) cardamom

Heat the water or milk with the spices. When it boils, turn off the heat and remove the cardamom or vanilla pods or cinnamon bark. Add the chocolate. Stir until it dissolves. Add sugar as needful (less is probably more 'authentic'), whisk and serve.

Venison Casserole

This old English dish involves the medieval combination of meat and spices, given depth by the addition of cocoa.

olive oil
2 large or 3 small onions
3 cloves of garlic

6 rashers smoked bacon or pancetta
1 kg diced venison
2 tbsp plain flour
300 g mushrooms
4 or 5 carrots
a glass or two of drinkable red wine
around 500 ml beef, chicken or vegetable stock
1 tbsp cocoa powder
a piece of cinnamon bark of around 5 cm
8–12 cloves, according to taste

In a deep casserole, fry the onions and garlic with the pancetta or bacon until soft and golden. Meanwhile, wash and slice the mushrooms and carrots. Remove the onions to a plate, turn up the heat and sear the venison with the flour in the pan until it is browned. Reduce the heat, return the onions, garlic and bacon to the pan and add the mushrooms and carrots. Sauté until the mushrooms begin to shed their liquor and then add the wine and enough stock to cover the meat and vegetables. Add the cocoa powder, cinnamon bark and cloves. Bring to the boil and then either simmer or place in a slow oven (around 130° C) for two or three hours, until the meat is soft but not falling apart. Serve with rice or baked potatoes and winter vegetables.

Chocolate Biscuit Cake

Another very English use of chocolate. Depending on the chocolate and the biscuits you choose, this can be as sophisticated or childish as you like; digestive biscuits and milk chocolate will produce something very different from stem ginger cookies or amaretti and a high-cocoa plain chocolate. For a mint version which, like the lavender pots, uses traditional herbs in an unusual context, omit the dried fruit and, before putting the cake in the fridge, spread over the top melted mint chocolate or chocolate to which you have added a few drops of peppermint oil.

300 g biscuits
300 g chocolate
100 g unsalted butter, cut into cubes
150 g chopped dried fruit, to taste (raisins are traditional, prunes work well, apricots or cherries would also be good)
3 tbsp brandy (optional)

If you are using the fruit, put it in a bowl and pour over the brandy. Put the biscuits inside at least two food-grade plastic bags and break them into a mixture of crumbs and small pieces with a rolling pin. Melt the butter in a large, heavy-based pan and add the chocolate, broken into pieces. Heat gently until the chocolate has melted. Add the broken biscuits and fruit to the chocolate and butter, stir well to combine and pour into a roasting tin, pressing the mixture down as necessary. This can be topped with more melted chocolate at this stage. Place the tin in the fridge to set.

Experimental Chocolate Truffles

As we have seen, making your own chocolate from raw ingredients is not a possibility in the domestic kitchen, but these are an easy way of exploring possible (and impossible) combinations. Made with any kind of chocolate, these can take any flavouring you care to experiment with: flowers (rose, jasmine, violet), spices (vanilla, cardamom, chilli), herbs (rosemary, lemon balm, thyme), fruit (citrus zest, crushed raspberries, mango pulp). You could also add coffee, almost any kind of spirits, aromatic teas or whatever else seems likely to work.

275 ml whipping cream
450 g chocolate

Put your chosen flavouring into the cream and heat gently. Turn off the stove and leave it to infuse until you have achieved the desired strength (probably around 20–30 minutes for more subtle flavours and rather less for chilli, coffee or pepper). Melt the chocolate, either in a bowl over simmering water or gently and carefully on the stove, and then pour the flavoured cream through a sieve into the melted chocolate. Stir thoroughly to combine, and place in the fridge for around fifteen minutes. Using a teaspoon, make small balls of the truffle mixture, which could be dredged with a good cocoa powder, icing sugar and/or spice. Return to the fridge to set, and eat within 48 hours.

Patrick's Guanaja Chocolate and Armagnac Mousse

This recipe comes from Patrick Williams, who runs the award-winning Patrick's Kitchen in The Goods Shed, a daily farmers' market and restaurant in Canterbury, England. Patrick makes and sells about four batches of this each week, and it is deservedly popular. A respectful use for really good chocolate!

300 g chocolate, 70% Guanaja or similar
300 g unsalted butter, finely chopped
6 medium eggs, separated
6 egg whites
70 g caster sugar
40 ml (a good shot) of Armagnac (optional)

Cautiously melt the chocolate and butter pieces over slow simmering water in a metal or glass bowl. When it is melted, take off the heat.

Put the egg yolks, 60 g sugar, splash of water in another bowl. Place this bowl over a pan of fast-boiling water and whisk the contents together until the mixture is pale and thickened. Remove from the heat, and whisk in the Armagnac. (The aim is to get the chocolate mixture and egg yolk mixture to a similar temperature for Step 3.)

Softly whisk the egg yolk mixture into the melted chocolate, mixing gently but thoroughly, including the edges of the bowl.

In a clean, dry bowl, whisk the egg whites (by hand or machine) with a pinch of salt. When they form soft peaks, add the remaining sugar and continue whisking. (The sugar helps the egg white to stiffen slightly.)

Lightly whisk a third of the egg whites in to the chocolate mixture to lighten it. Fold in the remaining egg whites carefully and thoroughly, taking care to lift the melted chocolate at the bottom of the bowl. (This maintains consistency across the entire batch.)

Spoon carefully into about 8 small ramekins, or one large bowl, and chill, preferably overnight.

Eat within a couple of days.

References

1 Sophie D. Coe and Michael D. Coe, *The True History of Chocolate* (London, 1996), p. 22.
2 Marcy Norton, 'Tasting Empire: Chocolate and the European Internalization of Mesoamerican Aesthetics', *American Historical Review* (June 2006), pp. 660–91.
3 Robert Latham, ed., *Diary of Samuel Pepys* (Berkeley, CA, 2000), vol. III, p. 182.
4 Marquis de Sade, *Lettres à sa femme*, ed. Marc Buffat (Brussels, 1997), p. 327 (my translation).
5 Deirdre Le Faye, ed., *Jane Austen's Letters* (Oxford, 1995), p. 243.

Select Bibliography

Books

Brown, Peter B., *In Praise of Hot Liquors: The Study of Chocolate, Coffee and Tea-Drinking 1600–1850* (York, 1995)

Clarence-Smith, William Gervase, *Cocoa and Chocolate, 1765–1914* (London, 2000)

Coe, Sophie D., and Michael D. Coe, *The True History of Chocolate* (London, 1996)

Cox, Cat, *Chocolate Unwrapped: The Politics of Pleasure* (London, 2003)

Doutre-Roussel, Chloé, *The Chocolate Connoisseur: For Everyone with a Passion for Chocolate* (London, 2005)

Foster, Nelson, and Linda S. Cordell, eds, *Chillies to Chocolate: Food the Americas Gave the World* (Tucson, AZ, 1996)

Harwich, Nikita, *Histoire du Chocolat* (Paris, 1992)

Knapp, A. W., *Cocoa and Chocolate: Their History from Plantation to Consumer* (London, 1920)

Lopez, Ruth, *Chocolate: The Nature of Indulgence* (New York, 2002)

Off, Carol, *Bitter Chocolate: Investigating the Dark Side of the World's Most Seductive Sweet* (Toronto, 2007)

Richardson, Paul, *Indulgence: One Man's Selfless Search for the Best Chocolate in the World* (London, 2003)

Satre, Lowell J., *Chocolate on Trial: Slavery, Politics and the Ethics of Business* (Athens, OH, 2005)

Schivelbusch, Wolfgang, *Tastes of Paradise: A Social History of Spices, Stimulants and Intoxicants* (New York, 1993)

Szogyi, Alex, ed., *Chocolate, Food of the Gods* (Westport, CT, 1997)
Terrio, Susan J., *Crafting the Culture and History of French Chocolate* (Berkeley, CA, 2000)
Young, Allen M., *The Chocolate Tree: A Natural History of Cacao* (Washington, DC, 1994)

Articles and Journals

Special issue on chocolate, *Food and Foodways: Explorations in the Culture and History of Human Nourishment*, XV (2007)
Few, Martha, 'Chocolate, Sex and Disorderly Women in Late-Seventeenth and Early-Eighteenth-Century Guatemala', *Ethnohistory*, LII/4 (Fall 2005), pp. 673–87
Laudan, Rachel, and Jeffrey M. Pilcher, 'Chiles, Chocolate and Race in New Spain: Glancing Backward to New Spain or Looking Forward to Mexico?', *Eighteenth-Century Life*, XXIII (May 1999), pp. 59–70
Norton, Marcy, 'Tasting Empire: Chocolate and the European Internalization of Mesoamerican Aesthetics', *American Historical Review* (June 2006), pp. 660–91
Prufer, Keith M., and W. Jeffrey Hurst, 'Chocolate in the Underworld Space of Death: Cacao Seeds from an Early Classic Mortuary Cave', *Ethnohistory*, LIV/2 (Spring 2007), pp. 273–301

Websites and Associations

Chocolate History

The Chocolate Research Portal
https://cocoaknow.ucdavis.edu/ChocolateResearch

Cocoa Reworks: Memories of Rowntree
www.cocoareworks.co.uk

Borthwick Institute, University of York
http://www.york.ac.uk/inst/bihr/guideleaflets/womens/women_doc6_rowntree.htm

Chocolate Campaigns

Stop Chocolate Slavery
http://vision.ucsd.edu/~kbranson/stopchocolateslavery/goodchocolateproducts.html

International Labour Rights Forum's Cocoa Campaign
www.laborrights.org/stop-child-labor/cocoa-campaign

Be Treatwise campaign
www.betreatwise.org.uk

Chocolate Firms

Amedei
www.amedei.com/jspamedei/index.jsp

Bloomsberry
www.bloomsberry.com

Bonnat
www.bonnat-chocolatier.com

Côte d'Or
www.cotedor.com

Seattle 'Chick chocolate'
www.chickchocolates.com

Tony's Chocolonely
www.chocolonely.com

Valrhona
www.valrhona.com

Acknowledgements

Thank you to Max and Tobias for patience in chocolate shops, and to Anthony for pretending to believe that all the chocolate was there for professional reasons.

Sarah Moss

Thanks to Linda McGavigan for kindly opening up her own private stock of chocolate lore from Trinidad; Margaret and Norman MacDonald for opening up their vast stores of knowledge; Frank Schipper and Judith Schueler for sharing bits of Dutch chocolate lore, Emma Robertson for pointing out (and creating) the cocoa reworks project; Sara Slinn at the Borthwick Institute in York for her help and patience with sourcing photos; Edith Badenoch for the cowboy cookie recipe.

Alexander Badenoch

Photo Acknowledgements

The author and publishers wish to express their thanks to the below sources of illustrative material and/or permission to reproduce it. Locations of some artworks are also given below.

Alvimann/MorgueFile: p. 88; A. Badenoch: pp. 82, 84, 91, 100, 104, 109; Alain Beguerie: p. 98; David Bernstein, New York/Werner Forman Archive: p. 10; Borthwick Institute: pp. 75, 112, 113; Bundesarchiv: pp. 38, 42, 83, 84; The image of the Black in Western Art Research Project and Photo Archive, W.E.B. Du Bois Institute for African and African American Research, Harvard University: p. 43; Godiva Chocolates: p. 70; Mary Evans Picture Library: p. 20; Michael Leaman/Reaktion Books: p. 66; Library of Congress: pp. 67, 79; National Museum of Anthropology, Mexico City/Werner Forman Archive: p. 19; Margaret F. MacDonald collection (*Die Praktische Konditoreikunst*, 1927): p. 97; Maceofoto/Istockphoto: p. 6; Edward H. Merrin Gallery, New York/Werner Forman Archive: p. 18; Montezuma's Chocolates: p. 71; Roger-Viollet/Rex Features: pp. 32, 49, 64; Sheila Terry/Science Photo Library: p. 16.

Index

italic numbers refer to illustrations; **bold** to recipes